John Millington Synge

Riders to the Sea

Edited by
David R. Clark
University of Massachusetts, Amherst
Assisted by Mary Adele Clark

The Merrill Literary Casebook Series
Edward P. J. Corbett, Editor

Charles E. Merrill Publishing Company
A Bell & Howell Company
Columbus, Ohio

For Rosalind, John, Ridgley, and Mary Frances:
In Memory of Aran

ISBN: 0-675-09307-4

Library of Congress Catalog Number: 79-124352

1 2 3 4 5 6 7 8 9 10—76 75 74 73 72 71 70

Printed in the United States of America

Foreword

The Charles E. Merrill Literary Casebook Series deals with short literary works, arbitrarily defined here as "works which can be easily read in a single sitting." Accordingly, the series will concentrate on poems, short stories, brief dramas, and literary essays. These casebooks are designed to be used in literature courses or in practical criticism courses where the instructor wants to expose his students to an extensive and intensive study of a single, short work or in composition courses where the instructor wants to expose his students to the discipline of writing a research paper on a literary text.

All of the casebooks in the series follow this format: (1) foreword; (2) the author's introduction; (3) the text of the literary work; (4) a number of critical articles on the literary work; (5) suggested topics for short papers on the literary work; (6) suggested topics for long (10-15 pages) papers on the literary work; (7) a selective bibliography of additional readings on the literary work; (8) general instructions for the writing of a research paper. Some of the casebooks, especially those dealing with poetry, may carry an additional section, which contains such features as variant versions of the work, a closely related literary work, comments by the author and his contemporaries on the work.

So that students might simulate first-hand research in library copies of books and bound periodicals, each of the critical articles carries full bibliographical information at the bottom of the first page of the article, and the text of the article carries the actual page-numbers of the original source. A notation like /131/ after a word in the text indicates that *after* that word in the original source the article went over to page 131. All of the text between that number and the next number, /132/, can be taken as occurring on page 131 of the original source.

Edward P.J. Corbett
General Editor

Contents

Introduction

Edmund John Millington Synge was born at Rathfarnham, County Dublin, Ireland, on April 16, 1871. He came of a well-known Wicklow family of Anglo-Irish Protestant stock. His father, a Dublin barrister, died in 1872. His mother, daughter of a rector, was very religious, and an uncle had been a Protestant missionary to the rocky, storm-beaten Aran Islands, off the west coast of Ireland—the scene of *Riders to the Sea*. Earlier ancestors were also connected with the church. Synge himself, however, renounced formal religion in his teens.

Interested in nature study, music, languages (including Irish) and literature, he studied at Trinity College, Dublin, and the Royal Academy of Music. In 1893 he went to Germany for further musical training (his instrument was the violin), but in 1895 he gave up the idea of a musical career and turned to the study of languages and of French literature at the Sorbonne in Paris. There he attended lectures by the great Celtic scholar H. d'Arbois de Jubainville—sometimes finding himself the only student present.

At the time of his historic meeting with the Irish poet William Butler Yeats, in Paris in 1896, Synge was an unknown, unpublished poet, translator, and critic. Yeats wrote an account of the meeting in a 1905 essay:

> He had learned Irish years ago, but had begun to forget it, for the only language that interested him was that conventional language of modern poetry which has begun to make us all weary. . . . I said: "Give up Paris. . . . Go to the Aran Islands. Live there as if you were one of the people themselves; express a life that has never found expression." I had just come from Aran, and my imagination was full of those grey islands where men must reap with knives because of the stones.
>
> He went to Aran and became part of its life, living upon salt fish and eggs, talking Irish for the most part, but listening also to the beautiful English which has grown up in Irish-speaking districts, and takes its vocabulary from the time of Malory and of the translators of the Bible but its idiom, and its vivid metaphor from Irish.[1]

---

[1] *Essays and Introductions* (New York, 1961), pp. 298-99.

1

Synge made five visits to Aran in the summers of 1898 through 1902. In all, he stayed more than four months on the islands.

During this same period the Irish dramatic movement was born. In 1899 the Irish Literary Theatre was started by Yeats, Lady Gregory, Edward Martyn, and George Moore. This was followed in 1903 by the Irish National Theatre Society, based on a company of Irish actors led by Frank and W. G. Fay. The latter was to play leading roles in most first performances of Synge's plays.

Synge had finished his book *The Aran Islands* by November 1901 although it was not published until 1907. In the summer of 1902 he had written *In the Shadow of the Glen* and *Riders to the Sea* and the first draft of *The Tinkers Wedding*. *Riders to the Sea* was first published in *Samhain*, an occasional review edited by Yeats, in September 1903. *In the Shadow of the Glen* was staged by the Irish National Theatre Society in Molesworth Hall, Dublin, in October 1903 and raised considerable opposition because of its ironically realistic picture of Irish life; and *Riders to the Sea* was staged on February 25, 1904, in the same place, but with much less excitement resulting. When, as a result of a gift by Miss Annie E. Horniman, the Abbey Theatre opened its doors December 27, 1904, Synge, along with Yeats and Lady Gregory, was one of the three directors.

The plays we have mentioned announced the advent of a new and remarkable talent. Then came *The Well of the Saints*, produced at the Abbey Theatre February 3, 1905, published 1905, and Synge's masterpiece, *The Playboy of the Western World*, produced on January 26, 1907, published 1907. The famous riots over *The Playboy* ended in triumph for the Abbey, the directors winning their point that artistic, not political, standards should guide the theatre, and Synge winning a world-wide reputation. He did not live long to enjoy it, however. He died in Dublin March 24, 1909, aged not quite thirty-eight years. His unfinished *Deirdre of the Sorrows*, the first of his plays to use material from the Irish mythological cycles, was performed at the Abbey in January 1910, after his death, and published in that year. His bereaved fiancée Molly Allgood (Maire O'Neill) played the part of Deirdre.

All his remarkable development had taken place in less than a dozen years.

Leaving George Bernard Shaw aside as peripheral to the Irish dramatic movement, one thinks of John Synge as the first of its dramatists, antedating Sean O'Casey, outshining Lady Gregory, and being pure dramatist, not poet turned dramatist as was Yeats. The essential dramatic quality which distinguished Synge from Yeats, the Irish lyric poet, and from James Joyce, the Irish prose artist, may be defined in terms of a famous passage from Joyce's *A Portrait of the Artist as a Young Man.*

> The dramatic form is reached when the vitality which has flowed and eddied round each person fills every person with such vital force that he or she assumes a proper and intangible esthetic life. The personality of the artist, at first [in the lyric] a cry or a cadence or a mood and then [in epic] a fluid and lambent narrative, finally [in drama] refines itself out of existence, impersonalises itself, so to speak. The esthetic image in the dramatic form is life purified in and reprojected from the human imagination. The mystery of esthetic like that of material creation is accomplished. The artist, like the God of creation, remains within or behind or beyond or above his handiwork, invisible, refined out of existence, indifferent, paring his fingernails.[2]

I doubt that Joyce had John Millington Synge in mind in this description of the dramatist. But the passage (whether or not it is the last word on the differences among the lyric, epic and dramatic forms) is quite close to Yeats's picture of Synge. There was in Synge's work a "furious impartiality, an indifferent turbulent sorrow,"[3] wrote Yeats after Synge's death. And it was through turning to drama and particularly drama of the life of the Irish country people, drama in dialect, that Synge was able to "refine himself out of existence" to purify the life he saw and experienced and to reproject it from his imagination.

Yeats writes that in 1898 having "settled for a while in an Aran cottage" Synge "became happy, having escaped at last, as he wrote, 'from the squalor of the poor and the nullity of the rich.' "[4] And he became a dramatist. An artist of Synge's type had to "take the first plunge into the world beyond himself, the first plunge away from himself that is always pure technique, the delight in doing, not because one would or should, but merely because one can do."[5] What Synge could do was to express the life of Aran in unique dramatic actions and dramatic speech. Synge became "consciously objective," Yeats says, through stepping out of himself into the Aran characters and the Aran speech. "Whenever he tried to write drama without dialect he wrote badly, . . . because only through dialect could he

---

[2] *The Portable James Joyce*, with an introduction and notes by Harry Levin (New York, 1947), pp. 481-82.

[3] *The Autobiography of William Butler Yeats* (New York, 1953), p. 317.

[4] *Ibid.*, p. 207.

[5] *Ibid.*, pp. 207-8.

escape self-expression, see all that he did from without, allow his intellect to judge the images of his mind as if they had been created by some other mind."[6]

In Joyce's figure the artist, like the God of Creation, has made a new world. Yeats, on the other hand, thinking of the dramatic artist as one whose piercing vision sees and recreates society, uses the figure of the Last Judgment, the Second Coming and the making of a new heaven and new earth. Rejecting "abstractions and images created not for their own sake but for the sake of party" the imaginative writer can "make pictures for the mind's eye and sounds that delight the ear, or discover thoughts that tighten the muscles, or quiver and tingle in the flesh, and so stand like Saint Michael with the trumpet that calls the body to resurrection. . . ."[7] So Yeats wrote in "J. M. Synge and the Ireland of His Time."

This quality of impartial and inexorable judgment appears in the style and technique of *Riders to the Sea*, with its simplicity, objectivity, bareness, and concentration. But it is also interesting that the very apocalyptic imagery which Yeats uses to describe Synge's work appears as a major image pattern in this play. Among the powerful Biblical allusions in *Riders to the Sea* are several from the book of Revelations or the Apocalypse. For example, in Revelations XXI:4-5 we read: "And God shall wipe away all tears from their eyes; and there shall be no more death neither sorrow, nor crying, neither shall there be any more pain: for the former things are passed away. And he that sat upon the throne said 'Behold, I make all things new.'" One of the disconcerting peculiarities of the life pictured in the play is that many of the objects that relate to the dead are brand new, whereas the living must be content with old things. Saved from the pig with the black feet—an image more terrible than Yeats's boar without bristles that roots the sun out of the sky—the new rope is wanted by Maurya to lower Michael's coffin into the ground if his body should be found, but is used by Bartley as a halter for the red mare which he will ride to his death. Bartley takes off his own shirt, heavy with the salt, and puts on a newer one, the shirt of the dead Michael. The most impressive emblem of newness is in the wide white boards meant for Michael's coffin but used for Bartley's. The spectre of Michael on the grey pony when Maurya sees it has "fine clothes on him, and new shoes on his feet."

---

[6] *Ibid.*, p. 208.
[7] *Essays and Introductions*, p. 316.

The red mare which Bartley rides and the grey pony on which Michael appears also echo Revelations, the description of the four horsemen of the Apocalypse. The grey horse is particularly relevant: "And I looked, and behold, a pale horse: and his name that sat on him was Death, and Hell followed with him" (Rev. VI:8).

But there is more to it than this. Given these hints one may find an extraordinary dimension added to the figure of Michael. See how Michael broods over the play from first to last! Maurya has been mourning him for days and the girls have too. He possesses their minds. Maurya is always going down by the sea to look for his body. The action of the bundle of clothes takes up much of the play. Michael's clothes hang in the corner. Maurya takes his stick to help her walk over the stones. Moreover, the grief for Michael is part of the chain of events that causes Bartley's death. Bartley insists on going to Galway in bad weather because now—Michael being dead—all the weight of responsibility for supporting the family rests on him, and this causes his own death. Maurya, possessed by the bitterness of Michael's death, refuses to return Bartley's blessing when he leaves against her will. (It is unlucky to make such a refusal to anyone who goes on a journey.) When, remorseful, she goes to the spring well to give Bartley the bread and return his blessing, the apparition of Michael on the grey pony frightens her so that she does neither. Finally, it is this pale horse with its pale rider that knocks Bartley into the sea. Michael is dead, and yet he is *there*. He becomes a supernatural presence overshadowing all the other characters and their actions.

The significance of this presence expands overwhelmingly when we consider the suggestions inherent in the names of the characters. Maurya, Mary of the seven times wounded heart. What other name could Maurya have? Bartley's is an ordinary name, the name of a mortal. He is the living son. But Michael is the name of an Archangel, the Prince of the Archangels, he who is like God. "And at that time [that is, the end of the world] shall Michael stand up, the great prince, who standeth for the children of thy people. . ." (Daniel XII:1). And in Revelations XII:7, we read "And there was war in heaven: Michael and his angels fought against the dragon. . . ." It is Michael who drives Satan out both in the original fall of the rebel angels and at the end of the world. Among the offices of St. Michael are these: (1) to fight against Satan; (2) to rescue the souls of the faithful from the power of the devil, especially at the hour of death; (3) to call away from earth and bring men's souls to judgment. In

Normandy in Mont-Saint-Michel (which Synge of course knew), St.
Michael is the patron of Mariners.[8] Some of these allusions are ironic
enough, but they are all relevant to the power of this image of
Michael in the play, a figure whom we the audience never know but
as a dead, yet somehow living, and therefore supernatural presence.
The effect is to underline the suggestions of classical fate with suggestions of Christian apocalypse—the terrible, more than the pious
aspects of it—and to help give this play the quality to which Yeats
referred in Synge when he said of him: "He was one of those unmoved
souls in whom there is a perpetual 'Last Day,' a perpetual trumpeting
and coming up for judgment."[9]

Yeats's general estimate of *Riders to the Sea* was very high. When
it was first published he wrote that it "seems to me the finest piece of
tragic work done in Ireland of late years. One finds in it, from first to
last, the presence of the sea, and a sorrow that has majesty as in the
work of some ancient poet."[10] In the preface to Synge's *Poems and
Translations* he praises the play's universality, "The old woman in the
Riders to the Sea, in mourning for her six fine sons, mourns for
the passing of all beauty and strength. . . ."[11] But Yeats does have a
specific negative criticism of the play. In "J. M. Synge and the Ireland
of his Time," he wrote, "I remember saying once to Synge that . . . I
liked *The Shadow of the Glen* better than *Riders to the Sea*, that
seemed for all the nobility of its end, its mood of Greek tragedy, too
passive in suffering, and had quoted from Matthew Arnold's introduction to *Empedocles on Etna* to prove my point."[12]

Empedocles on Etna is a tragic poem which Arnold withdrew
because in it and in other works like it

> . . . the suffering finds no vent in action . . . a continuous state of
> mental distress is prolonged, unrelieved by incident, hope, or resistance;
> . . . there is everything to be endured, nothing to be done. In such
> situations there is inevitably something morbid, in the description of
> them something monotonous. When they occur in actual life they are
> painful, not tragic; the representation of them in poetry is painful also.[13]

---

[8] *The Catholic Encyclopedia* (1911) x, 275-76.
[9] *Autobiography*, p. 311.
[10] *Explorations*, selected by Mrs. W. B. Yeats (New York, 1962), p. 106.
[11] *Essays and Introductions*, p. 309. Cf. p. 300.
[12] *Ibid.*, p. 336.
[13] Matthew Arnold, "Preface to the First Collected Poems," *The Strayed
Traveler, Empedocles on Etna, and Other Poems*, with an introduction by William
Sharp (London, n.d.), p. 291.

Arnold has said earlier that

> ... It is not enough that the Poet should add to the knowledge of men,
> it is required of him also that he should add to their happiness. "All
> Art," says Schiller, "is dedicated to Joy, and there is no higher and no
> more serious problem than how to make men happy." The right Art is
> that alone, which creates the highest enjoyment—. . . . In presence of
> the most tragic circumstances, represented in a work of Art, the feeling
> of enjoyment, as is well known, may still subsist; the representation of
> the most utter calamity, of the liveliest anguish, is not sufficient to
> destroy it: the more tragic the situation, the deeper becomes the en-
> joyment; and the situation is more tragic in proportion as it becomes
> more terrible.[14]

Is the play too passive in suffering? The action of *Riders to the Sea*
might be paraphrased: to persevere, against overwhelming odds, in
the face of constant and ultimate defeat, in the attempt to protect
and preserve and foster the family. This is the action that Maurya
has been engaged in for years and that Bartley, with his new responsibility, is just starting to be engaged in. I think that any of the little
actions will fall into this pattern. Cathleen's spinning is the attempt
to clothe the family—to provide yarn out of which to make socks
which will come back half torn off from the beaten bodies of her
brothers. Even the dropped stitches on the socks hint the ultimate
futility of human effort. Yet Cathleen returns to her spinning after
having examined the bundle of Michael's clothes. She bakes a loaf for
Bartley, forgets to give it to him; Maurya goes down to the spring
well to take him the bread and to give him her blessing, but fails to
do either. At the end of the play Cathleen is offering the loaf to the
men who will make Bartley's coffin. They are to eat it there in the
house while they work. Even the white boards represent a continual
and futile attempt. Bought for Michael, kept for Maurya, they are
finally all ready to be fashioned into a coffin for Bartley—but there
are no nails to finish the job. Someone will have to find some nails.

The new rope is bought to lower Michael's coffin, yet preserved
with difficulty from the pig with the black feet; then it makes a
halter for Bartley's red mare, which he rides to his death.

The girls try to spare Maurya's feelings by keeping the sight of the
bundle of Michael's clothes from her. Yet when she has seen the
ghost of Michael himself, Cathleen thinks it better to show her the
clothes to prove that Michael has a clean burial. But then the body

---

[14] *Ibid.*

of Bartley is brought in. Like the attempt to let Maurya have some sleep, the first thing that happens in the play, these efforts to protect Maurya are futile.

The action of Maurya in trying to keep Bartley at home or Bartley's action in insisting on going may equally be described as to persevere, against overwhelming odds, and in the face of constant and ultimate defeat, in the attempt to protect and preserve and foster the family. All the members of the family endure to the end. The plot line is very simple. What is left out, not what is included, is remarkable. For example, there is no young man around who has an interest in twenty-year-old Cathleen. That would be an interest in another family, another hearthfire; and the action here is to attempt to preserve this hearthfire.

The quality of Synge's achievement is shown by the way in which critics are concerned to demonstrate that this little play is not as tragic as Shakespeare or Sophocles. Thus Ronald Peacock says:

> As a tragedy *Riders to the Sea* is without doubt remarkable in the way it presents unpretentious heroism opposing Sea and Tempest that hang like Fate over men's lives. But it has nothing whatever of the complexity of the tragic processes in human life that we find handled and mastered by the greatest writers. *Riders to the Sea* is a fine piece of tragic art precisely because it does *not* compare with *Oedipus Rex* or the tragedies of Shakespeare. It is elemental, but also bare and excessively simple.[15]

Let us look at this simplicity. Plays are often described as having a three-part movement—the exposition, the complication, and the unravelling. Kenneth Burke, as Francis Fergusson interprets him, conceives a tragic rhythm of action from purpose through passion to perception.[16] Denis Donoghue explains this rhythm: ". . . The hero (or, if you prefer, the soul) moves from 'purpose' (the taking of a step, an attitude) through action or passion (the pain arising from action) to final perception, a new awareness."[17] But Donoghue does not think that *Riders to the Sea* follows this pattern: ". . . At any stage, the taking by Maurya of a positive course of action is impossible because the scales are too heavily weighted against her (a human conflict is one thing, but conflict between an old woman and the Sea is another). For this reason, action is frustrated, purpose cannot even

---

[15] *The Poet in the Theatre* (London, 1946), p. 92.

[16] Burke, *A Grammar of Motives* (New York, 1945), pp. 38-40. Fergusson, *The Idea of a Theater* (Princeton, 1949), p. 18.

[17] " 'Riders to the Sea': A Study," *University Review*, I (Summer, 1955), 56. Donoghue's essay appears on pp. 46-53 of this book.

be formulated. The play ends in Maurya's Acceptance, rather than in any positive perception."[18]

I feel, however, that the play does have the tragic rhythm. And certainly the scales are no more heavily weighted against Maurya than they are against Oedipus. Surely unalterable destiny is an even stronger opponent than the sea. In the first part of the play the characters do take various steps, various attitudes. Maurya is always either in her room seeking rest or on the seashore seeking the body of Michael or in the kitchen seeking to prevent Bartley from going to Galway—Bartley, her youngest son, over whom she can still seek to have some influence. At the same time, the exposition tells us that Bartley has determined to go. Meanwhile Cathleen and Nora take the step of hoping to identify the clothes in the bundle as Michael's and to keep the identification from Maurya. The complication or the passionate stage of the rhythm sets in when Bartley's and Maurya's reasoned purposes clash—Bartley goes off against his mother's will and Maurya refuses him her blessing. The two girls are impatient with the mother and in their impatience forget Bartley's bread. The attempt to improve the situation by sending Maurya to the spring well with Bartley's bread only worsens it. Maurya again withholds her blessing and also sees Michael's ghost, which throws her into terror. The girls' attempt to keep Maurya from knowing of Michael's death is foiled by Maurya's vision, which not only establishes Michael's death in her mind but also presages Bartley's.

This is the low point of the play. Maurya is sunk in despair. Of the optimistic young priest she says, "It's little the like of him knows of the sea. . . . Bartley will be lost now, and let you call in Eamon and make me a good coffin out of the white boards, for I won't live after them."

Maurya's attitude here is clearly too self-concerned to be tragic. What Donoghue says about the play as a whole is true about this passage. He quotes a modern description of the tragic experience by F. R. Leavis: "The sense of heightened life that goes with the tragic experience is conditioned by a transcending of the ego—an escape from all attitudes of self-assertion . . . the experience is constructive or creative, and involves recognizing positive value as in some way defined and vindicated by death. . . . Significance lies, clearly and inescapably, in the willing adhesion of the individual self to something other than itself."[19] Leavis here is getting at something of what

---

[18] *Ibid.*, p. 57.

[19] *Ibid.* Donoghue cites F. R. Leavis, "'Tragedy and the 'Medium,'" *The Common Pursuit* (London, 1952), pp. 131-32.

Yeats and also Arnold had in mind in talking about joy in the tragic close. Donoghue believes:

> On this basis "Riders to the Sea" does not constitute the tragic experience, for at least three reasons: firstly, because Maurya's Acceptance which ends the play has in it nothing of the positive "willing adhesion of the individual self to something other than itself"; secondly, because there is in the play no significant equivalent of "the valued," and thirdly, because in the final analysis the play does not give "the sense of heightened life." We may even add a fourth reason, that Maurya's sufferings are determined by forces which do not include her will or her character.[20]

Let us examine the final passage of the play. The cry is heard in the distance by Cathleen and Nora. The third stage of the play, the unravelling, the moment of perception, is beginning. As Maurya tells how Patch's body was brought to the door at some point in the past, Bartley's body is brought to the door in the present. At first Maurya is lost in a half dream, still in the daze which began with her vision of Michael's ghost. She confuses the deaths of Patch and Michael and Bartley. But immediately she snaps out of it and deals with the matter in hand. When Cathleen says that Michael has been found in the far north, Maurya has one of the most realistic speeches in the play. The old woman still has a strong grasp of reality: "There does be a power of young men floating round in the sea, and what way would they know if it was Michael they had, or another man like him, for when a man is nine days in the sea, and the wind blowing, it's hard set his own mother would be to say what man was in it."

This bitter speech is spoken still from the hell of Maurya's despair —the desperate state of a mother who has lived in perpetual uncertainty about the fate of her children. But the uncertainty ends at this point. The clothes are Michael's. The body is Bartley's. Maurya's struggle is over. "They're all gone now, and there isn't anything more the sea can do to me. . . ." Maurya's stature as a tragic heroine must be measured by the power of her opponent the sea and by the length of her struggle against it. In this, she is contrasted with Bartley, who, I think, must be played as very young, and who is so easily killed in one of his very first encounters with the sea. Maurya also stands at the opposite pole from the young priest with his easy piety. We are reminded of the end of *King Lear*: "The oldest hath borne most: we that are young/Shall never see so much, nor live so long." All the actions which were started earlier in the play are ended here. The

---

[20] *Ibid.*

bundle which was concealed from Maurya is now opened, and Michael's clothes are spread by Maurya over Bartley's feet. The body that Maurya has sought for nine days by the sea shore is found—but it is ironically Bartley's body, not Michael's. The sleep that Maurya was seeking in the opening lines will now come to her. "It's a great rest I'll have now, and great sleeping in the long nights after Samhain."

She sprinkles the Holy Water, but she is only half risen out of her hell of misery and self-pity, self-concern. Consider the cruelty and callousness of such lines as "And I won't care what way the sea is when the other women will be keening." But "*She kneels down again, crossing herself, and saying prayers under her breath.*"

Cathleen fills the pause by returning to the subject of the white boards. A page back Maurya has asked Cathleen to call in Eamon to make her a coffin. Now Cathleen speaks to an old man of his and Eamon's making a coffin for Bartley. The "fine white boards" of which she speaks in almost Homeric epithet, and the "new cake" they are to eat while building the coffin paradoxically fill the room with suggestions of the scene of potential life, the lively scene that will go on tomorrow while the coffin is being built. The sound of building should be a cheerful sound, a sound connoting new life. The newness that this building process will herald is the newness of Maurya's exhausted peace.

But there is another reason for calling attention to the white boards at this time. Mentioning them points up the fact that Maurya is no longer talking about her own death. She has risen out of the self-concern and self-pity which broke her for a moment, and now she stands up to deliver lines which have a very positive degree of that self-transcendence which Leavis and Donoghue require. It also appeals to a positive value—the peace of God which passes understanding. It is no longer just sleep which she has acquired. It is peace.

"They're all together this time, and the end is come. May the almighty God have mercy on Bartley's soul, and on Michael's soul, and on the souls of Sheamus and Patch, and Stephen and Shawn (*bending her head*); and may He have mercy on my soul, Nora, and on the soul of everyone is left living in the world." In these words another of the lines of action has its completion. Earlier Maurya, resisting Bartley's going, has refused to return him her blessing. Later she tries to give it, and the words choke in her throat, and she looks up and sees Michael's ghost. But now in the words "God have mercy on Bartley's soul" she frees him for his journey and frees herself from the tensions that went with her earlier refusal. The family is, in some ironic sense that is beyond bitterness, truly together now. The conflicts are over.

It has not been noted, I think, that the conflict between Bartley and Maurya does continue in the play to this point and does disappear when she now returns the blessing which she earlier refused.

But if that speech appealed to Almighty God, the final speech returns to earth and speaks with almost Homeric epithets again of "a clean burial" "a fine coffin," "a deep grave" and ends with a great commonplace about mortality. The simplicity of it, coming out of the intensity of her experience of bereavement is most impressive, and I find in these last two speeches the sense of heightened life which Donoghue seeks for in vain:

> Michael has a clean burial in the far north, by the grace of the Almighty God. Bartley will have a fine coffin out of the white boards, and a deep grave surely. What more can we want than that? No man at all can be living for ever, and we must be satisfied.

It is a heightened life which can endure so much.

Synge in the execution of this plot has succeeded in imitating the action he intended to imitate, and that action is a serious, complete and great one. It seems to me that the character of Maurya and the strength of her struggle must be measured by the length of time she held out against her great opponent. If there is too much passive suffering—not enough positive will in Maurya and her play—that is because Synge chose an action which is suffering, the action of enduring. The fault, then, if any, is in the aim and not the execution.

But if we judge by effect alone, I think we still have to call this little play one of the great modern tragedies because it has that effect of tragic catharsis which Aristotle described as the specific effect of tragedy: to rouse pity and fear in order to transcend them in a consciousness and concern which is no longer self-centered. The change of tone, in the last speeches of the play, from self-concern to universal concern, and the change of pronoun from "I" to "we"—"*we* must be satisfied"—signify the achieved effect of tragedy which Yeats described in another of Synge's plays as "a reverie of passion that mounts and mounts till grief itself has carried [one] beyond grief into pure contemplation . . . that tragic ecstasy which is the best that art—perhaps that life—can give. . . ."[21] "The persons upon the stage . . . greaten till they are humanity itself. We feel our minds expand con-

---

[21] *Essays and Introductions*, p. 239.

vulsively or spread out slowly like some moon-brightened image-crowded sea."[22] We are "carried beyond time and persons to where passion, living through its thousand purgatorial years, as in the wink of an eye, becomes wisdom."[23]

---

[22] *Ibid.*, p. 245.
[23] *Ibid.*, p. 239.

Riders to the Sea*

Persons in the Play

MAURYA, *an old Woman*
BARTLEY, *her Son*
CATHLEEN, *her Daughter*
NORA, *a younger Daughter*
MEN AND WOMEN

SCENE—*An Island off the West of Ireland* /31/

Cottage kitchen, with nets, oilskins, spinning-wheel, some new boards standing by the wall, etc. Cathleen, a girl of about twenty, finishes kneading cake, and puts it down in the pot-oven by the fire; then wipes her hands, and begins to spin at the wheel. Nora, a young girl, puts her head in at the door.

NORA (*in a low voice*). Where is she?
CATHLEEN. She's lying down, God help her, and maybe sleeping, if she's able.

Nora comes in softly, and takes a bundle from under her shawl.

CATHLEEN (*spinning the wheel rapidly*). What is it you have?
NORA. The young priest is after bringing them. It's a shirt and a plain stocking were got off a drowned man in Donegal.

Cathleen stops her wheel with a sudden movement, and leans out to listen.

---

* The text printed here is that of *The Works of John M. Synge* (Dublin: Maunsel and Co., Ltd., 1910) I, 29-52. A few readings from other editions are noted. "Riders to the Sea," copyright 1935 by the Modern Library, Inc., is published in the United States in *The Complete Works of John M. Synge* by Random House, Inc.

NORA. We're to find out if it's Michael's they are, some time her-self will be down looking by the sea.

CATHLEEN. How would they be Michael's, /32/ Nora? How would he go the length of that way to the far north?

NORA. The young priest says he's known the like of it. "If it's Michael's they are," says he, "you can tell herself he's got a clean burial,[1] by the grace of God; and if they're not his, let no one say a word about them, for she'll be getting her death," says he, "with crying and lamenting."

The door which Nora half closed[2] is blown open by a gust of wind.

CATHLEEN (*looking out anxiously*). Did you ask him would he stop Bartley going this day with the horses to the Galway fair?

NORA. "I won't stop him," says he; "but let you not be afraid. Herself does be saying prayers half through the night, and the Al-mighty God won't leave her destitute," says he, "with no son living."

CATHLEEN. Is the sea bad by the white rocks, Nora?

NORA. Middling bad, God help us. There's a great roaring in the west, and it's worse it'll be getting when the tide's turned to the wind. (*She goes over to the table with the bundle.*) Shall I open it now?

CATHLEEN. Maybe she'd wake up on us, /33/ and come in before we'd done (*coming to the table*). It's a long time we'll be, and the two of us crying.

NORA (*goes to the inner door and listens*). She's moving about on the bed. She'll be coming in a minute.

CATHLEEN. Give me the ladder, and I'll put them up in the turf-loft, the way she won't know of them at all, and maybe when the tide turns she'll be going down to see would he be floating from the east.

They put the ladder against the gable of the chimney; Cathleen goes up a few steps and hides the bundle in the turf-loft. Maurya comes from the inner room.

MAURYA (*looking up at Cathleen and speaking querulously*). Isn't it turf enough you have for this day and evening?

CATHLEEN. There's a cake baking at the fire for a short space (*throwing down the turf*), and Bartley will want it when the tide turns if he goes to Connemara.

Nora picks up the turf and puts it round the pot-oven.

---

[1] No comma here in *The Shadow of the Glen* and *Riders to the Sea* (London: Elkin Mathews, 1905) and other editions. [ED.]

[2] The words "behind her" appear here in other editions. [ED.]

MAURYA (*sitting down on a stool at the fire*).   He won't go this day with the wind rising from the south and west. He won't go /34/ this day, for the young priest will stop him surely.

NORA.   He'll not stop him, mother; and I heard Eamon Simon and Stephen Pheety and Colum Shawn saying he would go.

MAURYA.   Where is he itself?

NORA.   He went down to see would there be another boat sailing in the week, and I'm thinking it won't be long till he's here now, for the tide's turning at the green head, and the hooker's tacking from the east.

CATHLEEN.   I hear some one passing the big stones.

NORA (*looking out*).   He's coming now, and he in a hurry.

BARTLEY (*comes in and looks round the room. Speaking sadly and quietly*).   Where is the bit of new rope, Cathleen, was bought in Connemara?

CATHLEEN (*coming down*).   Give it to him, Nora; it's on a nail by the white boards. I hung it up this morning, for the pig with the black feet was eating it.

NORA (*giving him a rope*).   Is that it, Bartley?

MAURYA.   You'd do right to leave that rope, Bartley, hanging by the boards (*Bartley /35/ takes the rope*). It will be wanting in this place, I'm telling you, if Michael is washed up to-morrow morning, or the next morning, or any morning in the week; for it's a deep grave we'll make him, by the grace of God.

BARTLEY (*beginning to work with the rope*).   I've no halter the way I can ride down on the mare, and I must go now quickly. This is the one boat going for two weeks or beyond it, and the fair will be a good fair for horses, I heard them saying below.

MAURYA.   It's a hard thing they'll be saying below if the body is washed up and there's no man in it to make the coffin, and I after giving a big price for the finest white boards you'd find in Connemara.

She looks round at the boards.

BARTLEY.   How would it be washed up, and we after looking each day for nine days, and a strong wind blowing a while back from the west and south?

MAURYA.   If it isn't found itself, that wind is raising the sea, and there was a star up against the moon, and it rising in the night. If it was a hundred horses, or a thousand horses, you had itself, what is the /36/ price of a thousand horses against a son where there is one son only?

BARTLEY (*working at the halter, to Cathleen*). Let you go down each day, and see the sheep aren't jumping in on the rye, and if the jobber comes you can sell the pig with the black feet if there is a good price going.

MAURYA.   How would the like of her get a good price for a pig?

BARTLEY (*to Cathleen*).   If the west wind holds with the last bit of the moon let you and Nora get up weed enough for another cock for the kelp. It's hard set we'll be from this day with no one in it but one man to work.

MAURYA.   It's hard set we'll be surely the day you're drowned with the rest. What way will I live and the girls with me, and I an old woman looking for the grave?

Bartley lays down the halter, takes off his old coat, and puts on a newer one of the same flannel.

BARTLEY (*to Nora*).   Is she coming to the pier?

NORA (*looking out*).   She's passing the green head and letting fall her sails. /37/

BARTLEY (*getting his purse and tobacco*).   I'll have half an hour to go down, and you'll see me coming again in two days, or in three days, or maybe in four days if the wind is bad.

MAURYA (*turning round to the fire, and putting her shawl over her head*).   Isn't it a hard and cruel man won't hear a word from an old woman, and she holding him from the sea?

CATHLEEN.   It's the life of a young man to be going on the sea, and who would listen to an old woman with one thing and she saying it over?

BARTLEY (*taking the halter*).   I must go now quickly. I'll ride down on the red mare, and the grey pony 'll[3] run behind me. . . . The blessing of God on you.

He goes out.

MAURYA (*crying out as he is in the door*).   He's gone now, God spare us, and we'll not see him again. He's gone now, and when the black night is falling I'll have no son left me in the world.

CATHLEEN.   Why wouldn't you give him your blessing and he looking round in the door? Isn't it sorrow enough is on /38/ everyone in this house without your sending him out with an unlucky word behind him, and a hard word in his ear?

Maurya takes up the tongs and begins raking the fire aimlessly without looking round.

---

[3] I have changed "pony'ill" to "pony'll" to conform to the 1905 edition. [ED.]

NORA (*turning towards her*). You're taking away the turf from the cake.

CATHLEEN (*crying out*). The Son of God forgive us, Nora, we're after forgetting his bit of bread. (*She comes over to the fire*).

NORA. And it's destroyed he'll be going till dark night, and he after eating nothing since the sun went up.

CATHLEEN (*turning the cake out of the oven*). It's destroyed he'll be, surely. There's no sense left on any person in a house where an old woman will be talking for ever.

Maurya sways herself on her stool.

CATHLEEN (*cutting off some of the bread and rolling it in a cloth; to Maurya*). Let you go down now to the spring well and give him this and he passing. You'll see him then and the dark word will be broken, and you can say "God speed you," the way he'll be easy in his mind.

MAURYA (*taking the bread*). Will I be in it as soon as himself? /39/

CATHLEEN. If you go now quickly.

MAURYA (*standing up unsteadily*). It's hard set I am to walk.

CATHLEEN (*looking at her anxiously*). Give her the stick, Nora, or maybe she'll slip on the big stones.

NORA. What stick?

CATHLEEN. The stick Michael brought from Connemara.

MAURYA (*taking a stick Nora gives her*). In the big world the old people do be leaving things after them for their sons and children, but in this place it is the young men do be leaving things behind for them that do be old.

She goes out slowly. Nora goes over to the ladder.

CATHLEEN. Wait, Nora, maybe she'd turn back quickly. She's that sorry, God help her, you wouldn't know the thing she'd do.

NORA. Is she gone round by the bush?

CATHLEEN (*looking out*). She's gone now. Throw it down quickly, for the Lord knows when she'll be out of it again.

NORA (*getting the bundle from the loft*). The young priest said he'd be passing /40/ to-morrow, and we might go down and speak to him below if it's Michael's they are surely.

CATHLEEN (*taking the bundle*). Did he say what way they were found?

NORA (*coming down*). "There were two men," says he, "and they rowing round with poteen before the cocks crowed, and the oar of one of them caught the body, and they passing the black cliffs of the north."

CATHLEEN (*trying to open the bundle*). Give me a knife, Nora; the string's perished with the salt water, and there's a black knot on it you wouldn't loosen in a week.

NORA (*giving her a knife*). I've heard tell it was a long way to Donegal.

CATHLEEN (*cutting the string*). It is surely. There was a man in here a while ago—the man sold us that knife—and he said if you set off walking from the rocks beyond, it would be in seven days you'd be in Donegal.

NORA. And what time would a man take, and he floating?

Cathleen opens the bundle and takes out a bit of a shirt and a stocking. They look at them eagerly.

CATHLEEN (*in a low voice*). The Lord /41/ spare us, Nora! isn't it a queer hard thing to say if it's his they are surely?

NORA. I'll get his shirt off the hook the way we can put the one flannel on the other. (*She looks through some clothes hanging in the corner.*) It's not with them, Cathleen, and where will it be?

CATHLEEN. I'm thinking Bartley put it on him in the morning, for his own shirt was heavy with the salt in it. (*Pointing to the corner.*) There's a bit of a sleeve was of the same stuff. Give me that and it will do.

Nora brings it to her and they compare the flannel.

CATHLEEN. It's the same stuff, Nora; but if it is itself aren't there great rolls of it in the shops of Galway, and isn't it many another man may have a shirt of it as well as Michael himself?

NORA (*who has taken up the stocking and counted the stitches, crying out*). It's Michael, Cathleen, it's Michael; God spare his soul, and what will herself say when she hears this story, and Bartley on the sea?

CATHLEEN (*taking the stocking*). It's a plain stocking.

NORA. It's the second one of the third pair /42/ I knitted, and I put up three-score stitches, and I dropped four of them.

CATHLEEN (*counts the stitches*). It's that number is in it (*crying out*). Ah, Nora, isn't it a bitter thing to think of him floating that way to the far north, and no one to keen him but the black hags that do be flying on the sea?

NORA (*swinging herself half⁴ round, and throwing out her arms on the clothes*). And isn't it a pitiful thing when there is nothing left of a man who was a great rower and fisher but a bit of an old shirt and a plain stocking?

CATHLEEN (*after an instant*). Tell me is herself coming, Nora? I hear a little sound on the path.

NORA (*looking out*). She is, Cathleen. She's coming up to the door.

CATHLEEN. Put these things away before she'll come in. Maybe it's easier she'll be after giving her blessing to Bartley, and we won't let on we've heard anything the time he's on the sea.

NORA (*helping Cathleen to close the bundle*). We'll put them here in the corner.

They put them into a hole in the chimney corner. Cathleen goes back to the spinning-wheel. /43/

NORA. Will she see it was crying I was?

CATHLEEN. Keep your back to the door the way the light 'll not be on you.

Nora sits down at the chimney corner, with her back to the door. Maurya comes in very slowly, without looking at the girls, and goes over to her stool at the other side of the fire. The cloth with the bread is still in her hand. The girls look at each other, and Nora points to the bundle of bread.

CATHLEEN (*after spinning for a moment*). You didn't give him his bit of bread?

Maurya begins to keen softly, without turning round.

CATHLEEN. Did you see him riding down?

Maurya goes on keening.

CATHLEEN (*a little impatiently*). God forgive you; isn't it a better thing to raise your voice and tell what you seen, than to be making lamentation for a thing that's done? Did you see Bartley, I'm saying to you?

MAURYA (*with a weak voice*). My heart's broken from this day.

CATHLEEN (*as before*). Did you see Bartley?

MAURYA. I seen the fearfulest thing. /44/

---

⁴ "Half" is omitted in some editions. [ED.]

CATHLEEN (*leaves her wheel and looks out*). God forgive you; he's riding the mare now over the green head, and the grey pony behind him.

MAURYA (*starts, so that her shawl falls back from her head and shows her white tossed hair. With a frightened voice*). The grey pony behind him. . .

CATHLEEN (*coming to the fire*). What is it ails you at all?

MAURYA (*speaking very slowly*). I've seen the fearfulest thing any person has seen since the day Bride Dara seen the dead man with the child in his arms.

CATHLEEN and NORA. Uah.

They crouch down in front of the old woman at the fire.

NORA. Tell us what it is you seen.

MAURYA. I went down to the spring well, and I stood there saying a prayer to myself. Then Bartley came along, and he riding on the red mare with the grey pony behind him (*she puts up her hands, as if to hide something from her eyes*). The Son of God spare us, Nora!

CATHLEEN. What is it you seen?

MAURYA. I seen Michael himself. /45/

CATHLEEN (*speaking softly*). You did not, mother. It wasn't Michael you seen, for his body is after being found in the far north, and he's got a clean burial, by the grace of God.

MAURYA (*a little defiantly*). I'm after seeing him this day, and he riding and galloping. Bartley came first on the red mare, and I tried to say "God speed you," but something choked the words in my throat. He went by quickly; and "the blessing of God on you," says he, and I could say nothing. I looked up then, and I crying, at the grey pony, and there was Michael upon it—with fine clothes on him, and new shoes on his feet.

CATHLEEN (*begins to keen*). It's destroyed we are from this day. It's destroyed, surely.

NORA. Didn't the young priest say the Almighty God won't leave her destitute with no son living?

MAURYA (*in a low voice, but clearly*). It's little the like of him knows of the sea. . . . Bartley will be lost now, and let you call in Eamon and make me a good coffin out of the white boards, for I won't live after them. I've had a husband, and a husband's father, /46/ and six sons in this house—six fine men, though it was a hard birth I had with every one of them and they coming to the world—and some of them were found and some of them were not found, but they're gone now the lot of them. . . . There were Stephen and Shawn were lost in the great wind, and found after in the Bay of Gregory of the Golden Mouth, and carried up the two of them on one plank, and in by that door.

She pauses for a moment, the girls start as if they heard something through the door that is half open behind them.

NORA (*in a whisper*). Did you hear that, Cathleen? Did you hear a noise in the north-east?

CATHLEEN (*in a whisper*). There's some one after crying out by the seashore.

MAURYA (*continues without hearing anything*). There was Sheamus and his father, and his own father again, were lost in a dark night, and not a stick or sign was seen of them when the sun went up. There was Patch after was drowned out of a curagh that turned over. I was sitting here with Bartley, and he a baby lying on my two knees, and I seen two women, and three women, and /47/ four women coming in, and they crossing themselves and not saying a word. I looked out then, and there were men coming after them, and they holding a thing in the half of a red sail, and water dripping out of it—it was a dry day, Nora—and leaving a track to the door.

She pauses again with her hand stretched out towards the door. It opens softly and old women begin to come in, crossing themselves on the threshold, and kneeling down in front of the stage with red petticoats over their heads.

MAURYA (*half in a dream, to Cathleen*). Is it Patch, or Michael, or what is it at all?

CATHLEEN. Michael is after being found in the far north, and when he is found there how could he be here in this place?

MAURYA. There does be a power of young men floating round in the sea, and what way would they know if it was Michael they had, or another man like him, for when a man is nine days in the sea, and the wind blowing, it's hard set his own mother would be to say what man was in it.

CATHLEEN. It's Michael, God spare him, /48/ for they're after sending us a bit of his clothes from the far north.

She reaches out and hands Maurya the clothes that belonged to Michael. Maurya stands up slowly, and takes them in her hands. Nora looks out.

NORA. They're carrying a thing among them, and there's water dripping out of it and leaving a track by the big stones.

CATHLEEN (*in a whisper to the women who have come in*). Is it
Bartley it is?
ONE OF THE WOMEN. It is, surely, God rest his soul.

*Two younger women come in and pull out the table. Then men
carry in the body of Bartley, laid on a plank, with a bit of a sail over it,
and lay it on the table.*

CATHLEEN (*to the women as they are doing so*). What way was he
drowned?
ONE OF THE WOMEN. The grey pony knocked him over into the
sea, and he was washed out where there is a great surf on the white
rocks.

*Maurya has gone over and knelt down at the head of the table. The
women are keening softly and swaying themselves with a slow* /49/
*movement. Cathleen and Nora kneel at the other end of the table. The
men kneel near the door.*

MAURYA (*raising her head and speaking as if she did not see the
people around her*). They're all gone now, and there isn't anything
more the sea can do to me. . . . I'll have no call now to be up crying
and praying when the wind breaks from the south, and you can hear
the surf is in the east, and the surf is in the west, making a great stir
with the two noises, and they hitting one on the other. I'll have no
call now to be going down and getting Holy Water in the dark nights
after Samhain,[5] and I won't care what way the sea is when the other
women will be keening. (*To Nora*). Give me the Holy Water, Nora;
there's a small sup still on the dresser.

Nora gives it to her.

MAURYA (*drops Michael's clothes across Bartley's feet, and sprinkles
the Holy Water over him*). It isn't that I haven't prayed for you,
Bartley, to the Almighty God. It isn't that I haven't said prayers in
the dark night till you wouldn't know what I'd be saying; but it's a
great rest I'll have now, and it's /50/ time, surely. It's a great rest I'll
have now, and great sleeping in the long nights after Samhain, if it's
only a bit of wet flour we do have to eat, and maybe a fish that would
be stinking.

*She kneels down again, crossing herself, and saying prayers under
her breath.*

---

[5] Pronounced "Sow'in", All Souls Day, November 1, the Feast of the Dead,
thought of as the beginning of winter. [ED.]

CATHLEEN (*to an old man*). Maybe yourself and Eamon would make a coffin when the sun rises. We have fine white boards herself bought, God help her, thinking Michael would be found, and I have a new cake you can eat while you'll be working.

THE OLD MAN (*looking at the boards*). Are there nails with them?

CATHLEEN. There are not, Colum; we didn't think of the nails.

ANOTHER MAN. It's a great wonder she wouldn't think of the nails, and all the coffins she's seen made already.

CATHLEEN. It's getting old she is, and broken.

Maurya stands up again very slowly and spreads out the pieces of Michael's clothes beside the body, sprinkling them with the last of the Holy Water. /51/

NORA (*in a whisper to Cathleen*). She's quiet now and easy; but the day Michael was drowned you could hear her crying out from this to the spring well. It's fonder she was of Michael, and would anyone have thought that?

CATHLEEN (*slowly and clearly*). An old woman will be soon tired with anything she will do, and isn't it nine days herself is after crying and keening, and making great sorrow in the house?

MAURYA (*puts the empty cup mouth downwards on the table, and lays her hands together on Bartley's feet*). They're all together this time, and the end is come. May the Almighty God have mercy on Bartley's soul, and on Michael's soul, and on the souls of Sheamus and Patch, and Stephen and Shawn (*bending her head*); and may He have mercy on my soul, Nora, and on the soul of every one is left living in the world.

She pauses, and the keen rises a little more loudly from the women, then sinks away.

MAURYA (*continuing*). Michael has a clean burial in the far north, by the grace of the Almighty God. Bartley will have a fine coffin out of the white boards, and a deep /52/ grave surely. What more can we want than that? No man at all can be living for ever, and we must be satisfied.

She kneels down again and the curtain falls slowly.

Richard Ellmann

From 1902-1903*

*　*　*

[Joyce's] main literary association in Paris was . . . with his fellow-Irishman, John Synge, who arrived at the Hotel Corneille on March 6, 1903, and stayed for a week to sell out, having failed to get on in Paris. . . . Joyce soon found that Synge was not the silent man Yeats had described to him; evidently his silence was with the eloquent Yeats alone. He seemed to Joyce a great lump of a man who could not be argued with,[1] but since Joyce was equally doctrinaire they in fact argued a great deal. . . .

Synge had by this time begun to prove himself as a dramatist. At Yeats's suggestion he had given up his notion of becoming, like Arthur Symons, a critic of French literature, and had gone to the Aran Islands in 1898. Then, and during the summers from 1899 to 1902, /129/ he listened to the nuances of Aran speech, and found the material for four plays, including *Riders to the Sea*. He had shown this play to Yeats late in 1902, and Yeats, when he saw Joyce in January, had aroused his jealousy by praising Synge's play as quite Greek. During his short stay in Paris, Synge lent Joyce the manuscript of *Riders to the Sea*. No manuscript was ever read with less sympathy. 'I am glad to say,' Joyce wrote to Stanislaus, 'that ever since I read it, I have been riddling it mentally till it has not a sound spot. It is tragic about all the men that are drowned in the islands: but thanks

---

* Reprinted from *James Joyce*. New York: Oxford University Press, 1959, pp. 128-129 by permission of the author. © 1959 by Richard Ellmann.
    [1] Herbert Gorman, notes. (The papers of Herbert Gorman are in the Croessmann Collection in the Southern Illinois University Library.) Djuna Barnes, "Vagaries Malicieux," *Double Dealer*, III (May, 1922).

be to God, Synge isn't an Aristotelian.'[2] This corner Joyce had for himself, and he proceeded to point out to Synge the play's Aristotelian defects. In particular he objected to its catastrophe, because it was brought about by an animal (a pony) rather than by the sea, and to its brevity. It was, he said, a tragic poem, not a drama. He told Synge to make a lasting argument or make none. Synge protested, 'It's a good play, as good as any one-act play can be.' Joyce rejoined that Ireland needed less small talk and more irrefutable art; 'No one-act play, no dwarf-drama,' he asserted, 'can be a knockdown argument.'[3]

Did he really like the play so little? It does not seem so, for already he knew the final speeches of Maurya by heart, and a few years later in Trieste he took the trouble to translate the play. But he gave Synge no quarter and went on to expound his esthetic theories; Synge listened and said to him ungrudgingly, 'You have a mind like Spinoza's'. . . .[4] They parted amicably on March 13, respecting and disdaining each other.[5]

---

[2] Letter to S. Joyce, March 9, 1903. Permission to include extracts from the words of James Joyce has been granted by the Society of Authors as the literary representative of the Estate of James Joyce.

[3] Gorman notes.

[4] Letter to mother, March 20, 1903.

[5] Synge's notes to Joyce are at Cornell.

Maurice Bourgeois

From The Plays[*]

* * *

Synge's diptych of one-act plays is singularly illustrative of the two chief aspects of Irish country-life. _In the Shadow of the Glen_ dealt with pastoral Ireland; _Riders to the Sea_ is taken /159/ up with the sombre poetry of sea-faring life. It smacks richly of the Ocean and its saltness; and in its attempt to depict the marine atmosphere on the stage, successfully rivals with—nay, in our view, surpasses—the comparatively few plays in which this difficult experiment has ever been tried.[1]

The date of composition of _Riders_ has been already stated [1902-1903]. The piece was first performed by the I.N.T.S. at the Molesworth Hall, Dublin, on February 25, 1904, and has since then been acted all over Ireland and in English-speaking countries. Contrary to assertions often made, it has never been produced in Prague or Buda-Pesth.

The site of the play is pitched in "an island off the west of Ireland" —undoubtedly Aran. On wave-bitten, wind-swept Inishmaan Synge had perceived the awe-inspiring tragicality of the seamen's lives, with the shiver of peasant grief at the human toll exacted by the rapacious deep, and the agony of women young and old who can do no more than wait and weep at home. It was on his fourth visit to the Aran

---

* Reprinted from Maurice Bourgeois, _John Millington Synge and the Irish Theatre._ London: Constable & Co., Ltd., 1913; reissued. New York: Benjamin Blom, 1965, pp. 158-172.

[1] To speak only of the Irish school itself, we know only of two sea-tragedies: _The Racing Lug_, by "Seumas O'Cuisin," and _The Storm_, by Hugh Barden. See also Mr. Edward Martyn's Ibsenian play, _The Enchanted Sea_, published in 1902 and produced in 1904.

28

Isles that he heard of the case of "second sight" which has suggested the very imaginative title of the tragedy: "When the horses were coming down to the slip an old woman saw her son, that was drowned a while ago, riding on one of /160/ them";[2] and he had previously made miscellaneous observations about the islanders' way of riding,[3] the maternal feeling among the women,[4] the fisherfolk's continual dread of the sea,[5] above all about the natives' attitude towards death,[6] that have unmistakably gone to the making of the play.

It will be readily conceded that a tracing of the psychological process by which Synge welded together these many details into a harmonious whole, although a task of extreme interest, would be a somewhat hazardous reconstruction, given the lack of biographical information, and the absence of any *central* "source" as in the case of *In the Shadow of the Glen.*[7] Suffice it therefore to analyze the dramatic moments or stages and the elements of pathos in the finished play.

The thread of material action is easy enough to follow. The scene is the cabin of Maurya, a fisherman's aged wife, whom the sea has already bereft of her husband and four sons. She is awaiting news of another missing son, Michael. A "young priest" has just brought in fragments of clothing found on the body of a drowned man washed up far away on the coast of Donegal, for Maurya's two daughters to identify. They recognize them as having belonged to Michael, and conceal them in the /161/ turf-loft, "the way the old woman won't know of them at all," nor "be getting her death with crying and lamenting." They strive to dissuade their last brother, Bartley, who is about to put to sea in a terrible storm, from undertaking his perilous voyage to the Galway fair. But he remains obdurate even to the entreaties of his mother, who is yet ignorant of her other son's fate, and he departs on horseback without the old woman's blessing.

The dramatic interest here is not one of misgiving or ambiguity, for the moment Bartley goes we feel sure he will never return, and, as Maurya herself declares with terrible prescience, "when the black night is falling I'll have no son left me in the world." Indeed, it is every onlooker's immediate foreboding that the boards bought for Michael's coffin will serve for Bartley's. So great is the certainty that

---

[2] *The Works of John M. Synge* (Dublin, 1919), III, 222.

[3] III, 59.

[4] III, 111-12.

[5] III, 127, 164.

[6] III, 208-9.

[7] *Scattered* germs of the play are to be found in the Aran book (*Works*, III, 121, 122, 154, 156, 167, etc.)

there is not even the excitement of suspense; and the action, though it will ceaselessly and unobtrusively widen and advance without a jar to the logically fatal and indubitable conclusion, can hardly be said to be progressive.

This extraordinarily deep sense of inevitableness is, we dare say, the richest source of tragic emotion in the play. When Maurya hastens away to bestow her blessing on Bartley, and is prevented from doing so by her otherworld, "spaewife"-like[8] vision of dead Michael riding /162/ in attendance upon him, this dream, which she defines with Shakespearean abruptness "the fearfullest thing," but expresses our common and natural foresight of the gloomy end of the tragedy. From the slow beginning onwards, we have been more or less unconsciously "prepared" (technically and otherwise) for the revelation by Synge's subtle and stark realism, which causes the homeliest details to assume a fearsome and premonitory significance. Intimate, familiar things like the "young priest" who is only heard of, the ominous gust of wind that blows the door open, the turf for the fire in a corner and the clothes of Michael in another, the fine white boards from Connemara leaning against the wall, the forgotten "bit of bread" which Maurya takes to Bartley, the dropped stitches in the stocking, are but weird symbols of an overmastering doom. Seemingly trivial incidents become as it were dumb actors in a sort of *arrière-théâtre* which is in eerie unison wtih the human drama before us. Expectant anxiety and imaginative awe gradually steal over us; we have before long divined that our prevision is fulfilled; and yet, when Maurya reenters with haunted eyes, a lonely, stately figure as majestic as the sea itself, her disclosure comes to us, if not altogether as a surprise, certainly as an irresistible tragic shock.

It may be well to pause in this breathless drama to inquire into the exact nature and origin of Synge's conception of fate. In this /163/ little act we are confronted with an impersonal note of impending terror—a perception of power intense, irresponsible, unfathomable, consigning humanity to utter destruction. Truly are the characters in their unprofitable strife with the cosmic forces representative of what a contemporary French playwright[9] aptly terms "le drame des consciences et du destin." Their conflict with the Ocean makes them great because nothing stands between them and the fierce onset of ineluctable circumstance; it actually raises them to heroic proportions. Synge's fatalism in *Riders to the Sea* is a distinctly Pagan, hence artistic, fatalism. It is, to some extent, the conception of a

---

8 "Spaewife" is the Scotch for a woman gifted with second sight.
9 Henri Bataille.

destiny akin to the Anankè which overshadows the beautiful in the
Æschylean tragedy; it is also, in a way, the grim Celtic Ankou, the
Breton personification of death.[10] Possibly Synge derived his keen
mystical sense of doom from the modern German *Schicksalsdrama*,
with which he was acquainted; or, if a more adequate parallel be
sought for, from his favourite author Maeterlinck, especially in his
play *Interior* (1894)—which, it may be recalled, figures in translation
in the répertoire of the Abbey Theatre, where it was produced in
Synge's lifetime.[11] A profound and oft-quoted passage in *The Treasure
/164/ of the Humble* ("The Tragical in Daily Life") has it that there
is more real drama in "an old man seated in his arm-chair, patiently
waiting with his lamp beside him, lending an unconscious ear to all
the eternal laws that reign about his house, interpreting, without
understanding, the silence of doors and windows, and the quivering
voice of light, submitting with bent head to the presence of his soul
and his destiny," than in "the lover who strangles his mistress, the
captain who conquers in battle, or 'the husband who avenges his
honour.'" Synge's minimization of external action, his psychologizing
or interiorizing of the drama which, we have seen, animates even
things by some all-encompassing but wholly acceptable symbolism,
seems to be contained in this *locus classicus*. At the same time,
the differences must be pointed out. On the one hand, it is a far
cry from Synge's live, clearly-outlined, flesh-and-blood personages
to Maeterlinck's more or less sickly *pupazzi*—as Mr. Yeats beautifully
defines them, "persons who are as faint as a breath upon a looking-
glass, symbols who can speak a language slow and heavy with dreams
because their own life is but a dream."[12] In other words, Maeterlinck has only atmosphere; Synge has atmosphere plus characterization. Next, whereas Maeterlinck, in this and other plays of his,
would fain wholly spiritualize dramatic action, state its case in terms
of pure /165/ consciousness, hence make fate entirely immanent,
Synge, in *Riders to the Sea*, stays half-way, and retains a material
fatality that altogether transcends man. The sea is here identified
with doom and death; it is the sea whose formidable presence is felt
all about the play; the sea that lurks behind the stage; the sea that
throws with loaded dice in the game of human existence.

This undeniable Maeterlinckian influence remains therefore im-
material as compared with Synge's direct and vivid contact with the

----

[10] Cf. A. le Braz, *La Légende de la Mort chez les Bretons Armoricains*, new ed.,
chap. III.

[11] March 16, 1907. Cf. also *L'Intruse*.

[12] *Synge and the Ireland of his Time* (Dublin, 1911), p. 29.

dismal realities of Aran life. Death as he relentlessly perceived it
amidst his rude island environment passes through and purifies the
whole of his immortal little act. His sympathetic insight imparts to
him a sense of grave and overwhelming dignity that impresses one,
say, in Andreef's novels or in Hugo's epic tale of Gilliat's struggle
on the lonely reef with the implacable laws of Nature. He himself
confesses in the Aran book that he "could not help feeling that he
was talking with men who were under a judgment of death."[13] And
this acute realization by the islanders that the shadow of nothingness
is perpetually hovering about them finds its expression in Synge's
play as in actual Aran life in the half-savage, half-musical melopœia
known as the keen (*caoin*).[14] This lilted recitative, with all its
threnetic appeal, is another very impressive pathetic note. Irish playwrights know it well—/166/ witness the dirge in Lady Gregory's *Gaol
Gate*— and Synge the musician also fully grasps its dramatic efficiency,
for he will use it again in his *Deirdre*. Faintly it sounds from the
opening of the piece, like some "unheard melody" perceived by the
spiritual ear alone; but at the climax of the tragedy it rises and
swells in entrancing power, and mingles with the moan of the
Atlantic which one knows without words is dashing its surf beneath
the cabin walls. And, as we listen to the strange litany of Maurya
chanting the names of her dead men-children, we remember Synge's
wonderful observation as he returned from the burial of an old
woman in Inishmaan: "This grief of the keen is no personal complaint for the death of one woman over eighty years, but seems to
contain the whole passionate rage that lurks somewhere in every
native of the island. In this cry of pain the inner consciousness of
the people seems to lay itself bare for an instant, and to reveal the
mood of beings who feel their isolation in the face of a universe
that wars on them with winds and seas."[15]

The wail of the peasant women is renewed when, by a spectacular
and somewhat melodramatic stage-effect which may be thought the
one fault in the play, the corpse of Bartley is borne into the room.
But this slight mistake is amply redeemed by the singularly august,
almost Greek, solemnity of the play at the close. The /167/ lyrical
fervour of the lament now gives way to a note of resignation which,
instead of being bathetic as might be expected, actually heightens
and intensifies the tragic effect. Maurya's closing words of half-
heathenish, half-Catholic submission, "No man at all can be living

---

[13] *Works*, III, 216.
[14] Cf. III, 50-2, 212 ff.
[15] III, 52.

for ever, and we must be satisfied," do not mark an anticlimax, but on the contrary, a paroxysm of "exaltation" which lifts the protagonist, in her perhaps overstrained part, above the tragedy itself. The old woman, who is what Synge once styled the "strong central life,"[16] can now almost take pleasure in her last son's death: "There isn't anything more the sea can do to me;" now that the tale of her loss is complete, she at last secures the ultimate rest and resigned lethargy of a paralyzed heart.[17]

We would fain interpret this concluding note of restraint and ascetic renunciation—which does not in the least debar genuine sympathy for the distress of bereft Aran motherhood—as expressive of Synge's individual stoicism and, in Walter Pater's phrase, "aristocracy of passion." Synge, it must be remembered, ever and always remains a personal author. He told Mr. Pádraic Colum that the reason why he wrote *Riders to the Sea* /168/ was that he had personally begun to anticipate something of the sadness of old age and death. Yet this autobiographical element does not exclude the influence of two literary works which may have reinforced Synge's precocious sense of human annihilation, and, together with the scenes which he had witnessed in Aran, led him to compose a sea-tragedy.

The first of these external sources of the play, as indicated in a foregoing chapter, is M. Pierre Loti's *Pêcheur d' Islande*. Synge greatly admired Loti, and the novel—which he was re-reading about the time he wrote his two one-act plays and parts of the Aran book—was among the volumes which he had formerly borrowed in Paris from a circulating library in the Latin Quarter at the suggestion of his friend Mr. D. J. O'Donoghue. One may indeed detect a striking parallelism of subject, atmosphere and situation in the two works. Some details and sentences in Loti are quite in keeping with the keynote of Synge's one-act tragedy:

"Ces hommes primitifs avec ces grands silences de la mer qu'on devinait autour d'eux . . ."[18]

"C'était donc possible, c'était donc vrai qu'on allait le lui enlever, ce dernier petit-fils!"[19]

"C'était bien ce qu'elle avait deviné, mais cela la faisait trembler seulement; à présent que c'était certain, ça n'avait pas l'air de la

---

[16] A phrase which Synge once used in criticizing Mr. Stephen Gwynn's *Robert Emmet*, which was first written as a play. "It lacked," he said, "the strong central life." *Robert Emmett* was therefore subsequently re-written as an "historical romance" published by Messrs. Macmillan in 1909.

[17] We shall find the same acceptance of foretold fate in *Deirdre of the Sorrows*.

[18] Ed. Calmann-Lévy, p. 11.

[19] *Ibid.*, p. 17.

toucher. /169/ . . . Elle confondait cette mort avec d'autres: Elle en avait tant perdu, de fils! . . ."[20]

This last touch, the facts just recorded, and the general juxtaposition of texts afford proof positive of actual influence. Indeed this is the sole instance in which it may be asserted with absolute certainty that Synge was beholden to some one else, if not for the actual subject of a play, at least for the external incentive or stimulus that fostered and vitalized his own original Irish theme, and ultimately inclined him to its selection and treatment. On the whole, Synge's close intimacy with life in Aran remained a far more important factor in the genesis of *Riders* than M. Loti's literary influence. In other words, Synge in Ireland felt the tragedy of the sea just as Loti had felt it in Brittany. Add to this that *An Iceland Fisherman*, despite its descriptive beauties and psychological merits, and its all-pervading notion of an impending terror, is a somewhat lax and inorganic narrative, whilst *Riders*, the work of a genius unhampered by technical awkwardness, is remarkable for its pithy (some say excessive) condensation and swiftness.

The other analogue of Synge's play in European literature is Hermann Heijermans' Dutch four-act *Meerspiel, On Hoop van Zegen (The Good Hope)*. The original was published in 1900, and immediately obtained a success in Holland and in two different German versions throughout /170/ Germany. Then it was produced in a French adaptation by J. Lemaire and J. Schürmann at the Théâtre Antoine, Paris, on December 8, 1902, and subsequently (April, 1903) in London, in Miss Christopher Marie St. John's hitherto unpublished English translation, with Miss Ellen Terry in the part of the old fisherman's wife.[21] Synge met Miss Christopher St. John at Mr. W. B. Yeats's rooms often enough between January and April, 1903, but he was not in town at the time of the first performance, and anyhow, we have seen that *Riders* was then finished. In the Dutch play, as in *Riders*, the tragedy is made the deeper by the old woman's submission to—nay, acquiescence in—the decrees of fate; and the general theme, based on the universal fact that the sea is very dangerous, and earning one's life by it, very hard, is practically the same. But with this common inspiration the similarity ends; no particular resemblance of treatment can be detected; and on the whole, as the English translator herself avers,[22] "there is no way of proving Synge's indebtedness to, or ignorance of, *The Good Hope*."

---

[20] Ed. Calmann-Lévy, p. 67.

[21] *The Good Hope* has been revived in November, 1912, by the Pioneer Players, London.

[22] Letter to the writer.

This may be deemed an all too lengthy comment on this diminutive one-act tragedy. Tragedy it truly is; indeed it is "of a new order of tragedy altogether. It is, perhaps, not so much tragedy as a fragment of life"—one might almost say, in the hackneyed phrase, a /171/ "slice of life"—"set in the atmosphere of tragedy. Even as there is not water in a mist of the hills because it is all moisture, so there is not tragedy in *Riders to the Sea* because it is all tragical."[23] It is elegy all through, but elegy in a highly dramatic form. The reason why we have dealt with it at such length is that it is Synge's absolutely un-questioned and well-nigh flawless masterpiece, the one play by which the general body of his countrymen desire his memory to live. It strikingly exemplifies Synge's unique and felicitous blending of cosmopolitan literature and Irish social experience into a work of heart-rending universal appeal as well as of individual self-expression. His other plays, like *The Shadow of the Glen*, are perhaps more narrowly national, and on this score objected to; and perhaps it was a mistake to perform (at the time of the now historical row) the broadly human, hence generally accepted, *Riders to the Sea* as a curtain-raiser to the intensely Irish, hence ever-discussed, *Playboy*. Further, the little play illustrates Synge's uncompromisingly veracious and drastic realism—although he here presents a reality altogether destitute of "joy"—, his sense of the elemental and the dynamic, above all, his unsurpassed skill and craftsmanship, which match the play itself /172/ in its poignancy. *Riders to the Sea*, without in the least being, as it has been somewhat hyperbolically hailed by Irish and English judges, the greatest tragedy of modern times, remains one of the most remarkable achievements in British play-making, and a dramatic episode of exceptional human interest.

---

[23] Darrell Figgis, "The Art of J. M. Synge," *Fortnightly Review* (December, 1911); *The Forum* (January, 1912); republished in *Studies and Appreciations* (London and New York, 1912), pp. 34 *et seq.*, one of the ablest critical studies on Synge.

James Joyce

Riders to the Sea
by John M. Synge*

/258/ Synge's first play, written in Paris in 1902 out of his memories of Aran. The play shows a mother and her dead son, her last, the *anagke*[1] being the inexorable sea which claims all her sons, Seumas and Patch and Stephen and Shaun. Whether a brief tragedy be possible or not (a point on which Aristotle had some doubts) the ear and the heart mislead one gravely if this brief scene from "poor Aran" be not the work of a tragic poet.

* Reprinted from *James Joyce* by Herbert Gorman. New York and Toronto: Farrar & Rinehart, Inc., 1939, p. 258. © 1939 by Herbert Gorman. Reprinted by permission of the Society of Authors as the literary representative of the Estate of James Joyce. This is a programme note which Joyce wrote for a production in Zurich June 17, 1918.
[1] This may be translated "internal necessity." Joyce is thinking of the occurrence of this word in Aristotle's *Poetics*, Chapter IX, on the law of probable or necessary sequence as applied to the incidents of the plot. [ED.]

36

R. L. Collins

The Distinction of
*Riders to the Sea**

A peculiarly persistent contradiction has developed in the critical treatment of John Millington Synge. Despite the variety of opinion, both in time and kind, there have emerged certain uniformities: Synge's work is of a piece; he discovered late what he could do; creatively, he did much the same thing from his first to his last play —although here there is always recognition that *Deirdre of the Sorrows* differs in content, if not in manner, from the other plays.

Alongside this uniformity—and usually unaware of the contradiction involved—there has been a steady, if unequal, division of opinion as to Synge's greatest work. Most critics have chosen to think *Riders to the Sea* the apex, although there is a smaller group who place that play in a distinctly inferior rank to that of *The Playboy of the Western World*, or even *The Well of the Saints* or *The Shadow of the Glen*. This is not a mere matter of enthusiasm for a particular work—it is tantamount to a complete act of exclusion. To the admirers of *Riders to the Sea*, the other plays are good journeyman work, only here and there having the seal of greatness. To those who praise most highly one of the other plays, *Riders to the Sea* is mechanically good, but at its best a mere school exercise.

The contradiction arises out of the same people maintaining the two things—that Synge's work is unified, yet that one part is clearly set aside from the remainder. All the critics are aware of a distinction. But they do not try to analyze this distinction and they do not seem

* *The University of Kansas City Review*, XIII (Summer 1947), 278-84. Copyright, University of Kansas City, 1947. Reprinted by permission of *The University Review*.

to recognize further that the distinction so marked between *Riders to the Sea* and the other plays is present because there was a dichotomy in the man. Creatively, Synge was pulled towards two contrary objectives; in his memoirs there is evidence everywhere of this strain, but the struggle is not immediately apparent in the creative works. It is not present, that is, within the corpus of a single play. The struggle is there nevertheless: one side of Synge's nature finds expression in *Riders to the Sea*; the other side, in all the other plays.

In all the plays save *Riders to the Sea* the reader or spectator detects easily the thread that holds them together—that unifies them, that marks them as products of a single pen and a single attitude. Despite the obvious technical differences of *The Shadow of the Glen, The Well of the Saints, The Playboy of the Western World,* and *Deirdre of the Sorrows,* the view of life by the author is the same in all. The fear of all the characters is that life will be unfulfilled— beauty dies—the paralysis of old age creeps in. Martin Doul, Christy Mahon, and Naisi have a family likeness: they are all poets, all "fine, fiery fellows with great rages when their temper's roused"; and Pegeen, Nora Burke, and Deirdre have within them the same desire for a full and vigorous life. They are all hard women to please; the cry of each is essentially the same: Nora, "a long while sitting here in the winter . . . with the young growing behind me and the old pass- /279/ ing"; Deirdre, looking forward to almost certain death and recalling with anguish the seven perfect years with Naisi just concluding, "Woods of Cuan, woods of Cuan, dear country of the east!"; and Pegeen, standing proud and wretched with the life that had beckoned so ironically now closing around her, saying, "Oh my grief, I've lost him surely. I've lost the only Playboy of the Western World."

In all these plays the identification of reader and spectator is with the characters: in their fortunes, in their hopes and fear, he participates, and the plays stand or fall on the interest aroused by the characters.

In *Riders to the Sea,* however, the thread is broken and the play stands apart from the other work of Synge. Many critics have tacitly recognized this fact and some, indeed, have briefly suggested the measure of difference separating *Riders to the Sea* from the other work. Darrell Figgis says that "we know, and are vitally interested in, Macbeth, and his tragedy is poignant to us with a sense of personal loss. But we do not know Maurya thus. She is not a person to us. She is the soul of a mother set before a cliff of terror. We shudder for all mothers of Aran in her, whereas 'Out, out, brief candle!' comes to us

from a man whose magnificence won us." And L. A. G. Strong comments on the play's "steady, eternal rhythm, to which the actors
move like puppets, or creatures in a dream. They are fated, but it is
the eternal pulse of Nature that governs them."

But no one, I believe, has studied the problem closely, no one has
distinctly marked wherein *Riders to the Sea* is set apart from the
other plays, and no one has assigned the reasons for the isolated
nature of the play. These reasons Synge himself recorded, if unconsciously, in the notebooks of his visits to the Aran Islands.

In the record of Synge's first journey to Aran there occurs this
passage:

> On the low sheets of rock to the east I can see a number of red and
> grey figures hurrying about their work. The continual passing in this
> island between the misery of last night [when the islands were shrouded
> in one of their recurrent mists] and the splendour of today, seems to
> create an affinity between the moods of these people and the moods of
> varying rapture and dismay that are frequent in artists, and in certain
> forms of alienation. Yet it is only in the intonation of a few sentences
> or some old fragment of melody that I catch the real spirit of the island,
> for in general the men sit together and talk with endless iteration of the
> tides and fish and of the price of kelp in Connemara.

Homely touches of character—men sitting together and talking
endlessly of tides and fish and the price of kelp in Connemara—is
this not the basis of drama? And especially in Synge's peasant drama
is not this steady humdrum of life basically felt and undeniably
necessary no matter what bizarre events, what "variations from the
ordinary types of manhood," what wild sayings and ideas come into
the plays? That is, is it not necessary if the artist has for an intention
the desire to depict Life in terms of lives?

II

No one will deny that such a desire was Synge's in all of his plays
save *Riders to the Sea*. But in that play Synge sought, I believe, to
achieve a synthesis of the effect Aran had had upon him; in other
words, he attempted to put that "intonation of a few sentences," that
"old fragment of melody," which seemed to him the real spirit of
/280/ the islands, into creative form. A few characters were necessary,
for he chose the vehicle of drama, but they were, it seems to me,
deliberately de-humanized—and this fact accounts for the great gulf
separating *Riders to the Sea* from Synge's other plays.

There are, it is true, many realistic details offered in *Riders to the
Sea*, the clean white boards for the coffin, the bit of new rope being

eaten by the pig with the black feet, the stick Michael brought from
Connemara—in a sense, too many, for as George Moore said they
occasionally make the play seem little more than the contents of
Synge's notebook. Yet these details of life as it is lived in one poor
cottage Synge offers not for their everyday human values (as he does,
for example, with Pegeen's enumeration of things to be sent against
her wedding day in Jimmy Farrell's creel cart by Mr. Sheamus Mulroy,
Wine and Spirit Dealer, Castlebar), but for the brilliant light they
help to shed in the author's presentation of the spirit of the place.
And, if it is objected that humanity is surely present in Nora's cry—
"isn't it a pitiful thing when there is nothing left of a man who was
a great rower and fisher, but a bit of an old shirt and a plain stocking?"—or in Maurya's terrifying "I've seen the fearfulest thing any
person has seen since the day Bride Dara seen the dead man with the
child in his arms," even these are unearthly wails that can be identified with the music that is implicit in Synge's conception of the spirit
of the place. Their burden, though expressed by human beings here,
is the same as that note Synge kept hearing in the cormorants over
the islands: "There is one plaintive note which they take up in the
middle of their usual babble, and pass on from one to another along
the cliff with a sort of inarticulate wail, as if they remembered for
an instant the horror of the mist."

Synge's character delineation in *Riders to the Sea*, like that in all
his plays, is that of the notebook writer. He observed life closely,
jotted down his impressions, and then he refined these impressions—
omitting all that seemed irrelevant, converting the individual to the
universal, and making all speech both articulate and memorable. But
the characters in *Riders to the Sea* end—I think deliberately—by
being bloodless creations.

Following the description of the dangerous exertions that are required of the Aran men merely to launch and land one of their
curraghs safely, Synge says, "This continual danger, which can only
be escaped by extraordinary dexterity, has had considerable influence
on the local character, as the waves have made it impossible for
clumsy, foolhardy, or timid men to live on these islands."

In the re-created play Synge's deft use of his observation and conclusion may be seen. For, despite the fact that all the men in Maurya's
family, up to and at last including Bartley, have lost their battle to the
sea, neither the reader nor the spectator ever thinks of any of them
as having been "clumsy, foolhardy, or timid." Certainly not "timid,"
because they live out their lives in the face of repeated warnings. Not
"clumsy," despite the awkwardness of a riderless pony knocking man
and horse into the sea, for Bartley is here combatting a supernatural

force. The hand of Fate is on him doubly: he leaves without his mother's blessing and her vision has foretold the event. And not "foolhardy," despite the attempts /281/ of Maurya to prevent Bartley from going on the sea, for the young priest has not forbade the trip, and the economic motive driving Bartley is strong: "This is the one boat going for two weeks, and the fair will be a good fair for horses I heard them saying below."

But after this is said and after we are aware how successful Synge has been in transferring from notebook to play this sense of extraordinary stoical character in the figure of Bartley, we must yet notice the significant hiatuses in the drama in this connection. Bartley answers no questions put by his mother, he offers only the explanation of the fair for the necessity of his journey, he does not defend himself against her pleas, he does not try to soften his departure. It is true that to Maurya's question, "Isn't it a hard and cruel man won't hear a word from an old woman, and she holding him from the sea?" Cathleen offers the argument of necessity and inevitability that "It's the life of a young man to be going on the sea, and who would listen to an old woman with one thing, and she saying it over?" It is true, also, that after Bartley's abrupt departure Cathleen indicates that he turned back for a moment at the door dumbly seeking Maurya's blessing.

But this is all that Synge attempts or allows in the matter of human relationships when there was room for so much. And the omission is due, I believe, not so much to the desired economy, certainly not to hasty writing but to the fact that Synge is dealing here not with people but with abstractions. It is the spirit of loneliness, of continual struggle ending only in death, of stoical acceptance of defeat that *Riders to the Sea* is to embody. The theme, the picture, the language are everything; the people are nothing. They hardly achieve even the abstraction of being the Mother, the Son, the Daughter. In *The Shadow of the Glen*, as in *Lear*, pity naturally accompanies the other emotions; in *Riders to the Sea*, in a situation potentially more pathetic, there is only dry-eyed despair and this arises out of our witnessing a crystallized moment in time and space and not out of sympathy with the characters.

At the close of the first of the Aran notebooks, written just after Synge had left the islands when, standing on the Galway shore, he could look across the bay to the islands and attempt an evaluation of his recent experiences, this insight appears:

> I have come out of an hotel full of tourists and commercial travellers, to stroll along the edge of Galway bay, and look out in the direction of the islands. The sort of yearning I feel towards those lonely rocks

is indescribably acute. This town, that is usually so full of wild human interest, seems in my present mood a tawdry medley of all that is crudest in modern life.

One may surmise that in such a mood as this *Riders to the Sea* was written. It is instructive to note that the "wild human interest," so much a part of *The Shadow of the Glen, The Well of the Saints, Deirdre of the Sorrows,* and *The Playboy of the Western World*— being specifically mentioned in the Preface to the last named play as a necessity for imaginative drama—at times is definitely antipathetic to Synge. His yearning at this moment is not to the people of Aran but "to those lonely rocks," as it was, I believe, throughout the composition of *Riders to the Sea.*

The characters of *Riders to the Sea* are made a race apart. Although Synge succeeds in making them symbolic of /282/ an everlasting struggle between man and natural forces, of man's fortitude and capacity for endurance, of man's dignity in the face of suffering, he does not attempt to individualize, to humanize, to provide them with the little touches that make created characters lifelike.

In most of the plays Synge's method of incorporating vivid details from the notebooks was to associate them with character—usually successfully, occasionally so that they protruded. There is the Tramp in *The Shadow of the Glen,* for example—a man who has lived his life in the back hills, with the mists and the storms, "walking round in the long nights . . . the time a little stick would seem as big as your arm, and a rabbit as big as a bay horse, and a stack of turf as big as a towering church in the city of Dublin." A man of courage, yes, but also a man who knows of things that cannot be explained rationally. He is willing enough to sit with Nora's "dead" husband at her request, but he is wise enough to take precautions against evil: "Maybe if you'd a piece of grey thread and a sharp needle—there's great safety in a needle, lady of the house—I'd be putting a little stitch here and there in my old coat, the time I'll be praying for his soul, and it going up naked to the saints of God." In Inishmaan the old story-teller, Pat Dirane, had told Synge of the efficacy of having a sharp needle on his person to ward off harm from the fairies, and Synge had noted that "Iron is a common talisman with barbarians, but in this case the idea of exquisite sharpness was probably present also, and, perhaps, some feeling for the sanctity of the instrument of toil, a folk-belief that is common in Brittany."

In contrast, there is Martin Doul, with his eyesight restored, grumbling at the amount of work being put upon him by his present master, Timmy the smith, and accusing him of all kinds of cruelty: "Oh, God help me! I've heard tell you stripped the sheet from your wife and you putting her down into the grave, and that there isn't the like of you for plucking your living ducks, the short days, and leaving them running around in their skins, in the great rains and the cold." Now, this recollection of Synge's having seen in a cottage in Inishmaan "all the women down on their knees plucking the feathers from live ducks and geese" is vivid, even more so than the original incident, perhaps justifies itself because of that fact, is appropriate enough for the sharp-tongued Martin, but is woefully inappropriate when applied to the brawny Timmy who would never be doing woman's work.

But the fact to be noted in both these examples is that Synge makes a conscious effort—here and again and again in the plays—to relate incident to character, to focus sharply the characteristic trait. In *Riders to the Sea*, however, the normal, expected human traits are not present. And in great part they are not present because Synge, having been impressed by the isolation of Aran and the resultant other-worldliness of its inhabitants, attempted in this play to record their distinction from ordinary folk. But Synge's method was not to display differences in personality between the islanders and other people; instead he almost completely denied all personality and individuality in favor of depicting the forces that governed the lives of these people.

When Synge was on his way back to Aran for his second visit, he met the boy Michael, his guide around Inish- /283/ maan on the first visit. Michael was now living and working on the mainland; and Synge "was singularly struck with the refinement of his nature, which has hardly been influenced by his new life, and the townsmen and sailors he has met with." Later in the day, Synge, Michael, and a friend of Michael's sat outside near the sea. "The day was unbearably sultry, and the sand and sea near us were crowded with half-naked women, but neither of the young men seemed to be aware of their presence. Before we went back to the town a man came out to ring a young horse on the sand close to where we were lying, and then the interest of my companions was intense." Imagine Christy, Martin Doul, even Naisi and the Tramp being indifferent to the women. But only by an act of will can Bartley, or for that matter Nora and Cathleen, be thought of in terms of romantic love. Passion there is in the young men—but it is expressed in terms of the fairly primitive struggle between man and horse. So also in *Riders to the Sea*. The emphasis lies here because Synge had been thus impressed time after time by the lives of the islanders. Human relationships on the island, when described at all, are always portrayed in terms of violence—the fierce mother love, the wild scorn of the girls for Synge when they learn he is a bachelor, the violent games of the young men and girls. And violence, while never an actuality before the spectator in *Riders to the Sea,* is omnipresent: it is the unseen force that governs the lives of the characters and accounts for the unceasing tension of the play. Certainly there are wild, free actions in all the plays, but in all except *Riders to the Sea* the violence arises out of character, or the action of character upon character. In *Riders to the Sea* it is the thing itself—crystallized and separated from its source of origin as from the people it affects. The characters serve only to identify and to concentrate attention upon the abstract force.

Perhaps it goes without saying that in the subordinate characters of the children and the neighbors who bring in the body of Bartley and fall into a deliberate frieze of grief around the apron of the stage, it is easy to see and to say that lifelikeness is sacrificed in favor of the abstraction. But what of the central character of Maurya? Is she too in a sense unhuman?

When Synge returned to Inishmaan for the second time, he lived again with the family he had visited on his first trip. He found changes in the household; Michael was working on the mainland, another son had gone to America. Synge was shown a letter from the latter saying that he was leaving New York to take up his life a few hundred miles inland—a letter that gave great grief to the mother, for "when she hears them talking of railroads and inland cities where there is no sea, things she cannot understand, it comes home to her that her son is gone forever. . . . The maternal feeling is so powerful in these islands that it gives a life of torment to the women. Their sons grow up to be banished as soon as they are of age, or live here in continual danger on the sea; their daughters go away also, or are worn out in their youth with bearing children that grow up to harass them in their own turn a little later."

No one will deny that this maternal feeling is strong in Maurya—no one fails to grasp the torment her life has been in the loss one after the other of her husband and sons. But, as Synge /284/ directs the course of the play, the torment is in retrospect—Nora, indeed, being amazed at her mother's calm acceptance of new disaster. The magnificent speeches of Maurya at the close of the play do not plumb emotional depths—nor were they intended to. They are not the direct lament of "Absalom! Oh, my son Absalom!" or the five-fold "never" of Lear; they are the circumscribed grief of one in sackcloth and ashes—mourning in a prescribed, ritualistic manner. Cathleen offers a natural reason for her mother's passivity—"An old woman will be soon tired with anything she will do, and isn't it nine days herself is after crying and keening, and making great sorrow in the house?"— but the true explanation lies elsewhere. It is to be found in the rigid control Synge exercised over the play, constantly forcing consideration away from Maurya and her troubles, and on to the spirit of strength, fortitude, and resignation that comes from constant conflict with the overpowering forces of wind and wave.

And as Maurya is the distinct center of the play, so the core of Maurya and hence of the play is this composite of qualities—violence, grief, endurance, strength, resignation—that for Synge spelled Aran. In all his other plays Synge sought to express his requisites of drama, *reality* and *joy*, in terms of people; in *Riders to the Sea* he attempted and achieved an essence. He put into creative terms what he had seen and, as an artist, been deeply affected by: "The whole sight of wild islands and sea was as clear and cold and brilliant as what one sees in a dream, and alive with singularly severe glory that is in the character of the place."

Denis Donoghue

Synge: "Riders to the Sea": A Study*

In "The Aran Islands", after Synge has described the keening at the burial of the old woman, he notes:

> "Before they covered the coffin an old man kneeled down by the grave and repeated a simple prayer for the dead.
>
> "There was an irony in these words of atonement and Catholic belief spoken by voices that were still hoarse with the cries of pagan desperation."[1]

This relationship between "Catholic" and "Pagan" becomes one of the most significant of the dramatic tensions established within the context of "Riders to the Sea": the tension between orthodox, institutional religion and the implacable power of the Sea.

In the first moments of the play, the words "God" and "priest" are mentioned:

> CATHLEEN: "She's lying down, God help her . . ."[2]

and then:

> NORA: "The young priest is after bringing them. It's a shirt and a plain stocking were got off a drowned man in Donegal."

Synge is here fixing the spiritual orthodoxy of his characters, establishing the religious, Catholic associations of the people:

---

* Reprinted from *University Review*, I (Summer, 1955), 52-58, by permission of the journal and the author.

1 John Millington Synge, *The Aran Islands*, with drawings by Jack B. Yeats (Dublin, 1907), p. 40.

2 All quotations from "Riders to the Sea" are from *Plays by John M. Synge* (London, 1949).

> CATHLEEN: "Did you ask him would he stop Bartley going this day with the horses to the Galway fair?"
>
> NORA: " 'I won't stop him,' says he; 'but let you not be afraid. Herself does be saying prayers half through the night, and the Almighty God won't leave her destitute,' says he, 'with no son living.' "

The priest's words come as if with an assumption of their right to exist in their comfort: even at this late stage in the family's sorrow, his easy optimism is received with no sneer. The religious associations are continued in the ritual of the Holy Water sprinkled on the body of Bartley taken from the sea. Throughout the play, the basic symbolic awareness is of the tension between Religion ("God", "young priest", "by the grace of God", "Holy Water") and the silent power of the Sea. This tension, implicit throughout, is dissolved into Christian Acceptance by its clear, agonised statement in the climax of the play: /53/

> NORA: "Didn't the young priest say the Almighty God won't leave her destitute with no son living?"
>
> MAURYA: "It's little the like of him knows of the sea . . ."

Here the sudden confrontation of easy, spiritual comfort by the clear facts of the case is intensified in its significance by the feeling that not even the power of "Almighty God" is enough to control the appetite of the Sea. The implications are unmistakable: Good (God) has none of the positive power or obvious existence of Evil (the Sea).

But thereafter, as soon as the conflict of Faith is stated, it is resolved by that "grace of God" mentioned so often in the play. Maurya's last words are:

> "They're all together this time, and the end is come. May the Almighty God have mercy on Bartley's soul, and on Michael's soul, and on the souls of Seamus and Patch, and Stephen and Shawn; and may He have mercy on my soul, Nora, and on the soul of everyone is left living in the world. . . . Michael has a clean burial in the far north, by the grace of the Almighty God. Bartley will have a fine coffin out of the white boards, and a deep grave surely. What more can we want than that? No man at all can be living for ever, and we must be satisfied."

"The end is come" has its human association with the idea of the community of the family, "they're all together this time," but its secondary implications are those of the Passion of Christ, "Es ist vollbracht," "It is consumated". The sacrifice is over.

The thematic situation of the play derives from the inhuman power of the Sea, and Synge has placed before the eyes of his audience a representation of sea-death in the white boards standing by the wall of the cottage. The new boards are there from the beginning of the play and they are to be made into a coffin for Michael, then for Maurya: they stand there throughout the drama and are finally used to give Bartley his "deep grave". The boards are therefore a continuously operative symbol of the presence of death. Maurya, after her vision of the dead Michael, says:

> "Bartley will be lost now, and let you call in Eamon and make me a good coffin out of the white boards, for I won't live after them",

and she remembers that one plank held the dead bodies of her sons Stephen and Shawn. When Bartley is carried up on a plank, Cathleen asks an older man to make a coffin, and here the white boards take on the clear implications of the death of Christ:

> CATHLEEN: "Maybe yourself and Eamon would make a coffin when the sun rises. We have fine white boards herself bought, God help her, thinking Michael would be found, and I have a new cake you can eat while you'll be working."
>
> OLD MAN: "Are there nails with them?"
>
> CATHLEEN: "There are not, Colum; we didn't think of the nails." /54/
>
> ANOTHER MAN: "It's a great wonder she wouldn't think of the nails, and all the coffins she's seen made already."

This is one of the moments in the play in which the purely human suffering of Maurya and her family is related to the religious orthodoxy within which they live. The Crucifixion is here a kind of middle event between the death of Bartley and the force which caused that death, a force which has no human associations whatever.

The Sea is, of course, the agent of the drama. Synge sets the scene in "an island off the West of Ireland" and the play, as seen through the eyes of Maurya, is full of the vision of life as a small area (the family) entirely surrounded by evil (the Sea). To Maurya the Sea is the Enemy, the destructive principle, destroyer of human and family continuity:

> MAURYA: "There was Sheamus and his father, and his own father again were lost in a dark night, and not a stick or sign was seen of them when the sun went up. There was Patch after was drowned out of a curragh that turned over. . . ."

Here two sentences from "The Aran Islands" present themselves:

> "On these islands the women live only for their children" (p. 62) . . . "The maternal feeling is so powerful on these islands that it gives a life of torment to the women" (p. 84).

To Bartley, however, the issue is not as clear-cut. When his mother opposes his going on the sea to the fair, he answers:

> "This is the one boat going for two weeks or beyond it, and the fair will be a good fair for horses, I heard them saying below",

but there is a much deeper force urging him. "Men who follow the sea have often a deep love for that hard life, which no catalogue of its practical virtues can account for. But in their dangerous calling they feel secure. . . . Waters and ships, heaven and storm and harbor, somehow contain the symbols through which they see meaning and sense in the world, a 'justification', as we call it, of trouble, a unified conception of life whereby it can be rationally lived."[3] This is the real urge, natural and moral rather than protective. The Sea represents the only terms in which Bartley can live with a purpose: the Sea is his life as well as his livelihood. The issue between Maurya and the Sea, therefore, is not merely a straight fight between Good and Evil for the soul of Man: the Sea may be Evil but it constitutes Bartley's only way of real life: to stay at home, to side with Maurya, would be for Bartley the yielding up of the source of meaningful living. For this reason, only one conclusion is possible when Maurya's appeal to Bartley is made on merely human terms: one set of personal values is confronted with another, and the individual (Bartley) must be guided by his own sense of life. Maurya's appeal interferes with an act that has a potent ritual value. From this angle, therefore, Bartley's death /55/ may be seen as "image of fulfilment (the 'entelechial' motive), in accordance with the double meaning of the word 'end', to name either the *purpose* or the *cessation* of an act. The 'logic of a life' can thus be represented by whatever way of dying is felt to be the fitting culmination of such a life".[4]

These values cannot, of course, be appreciated by Maurya, the Mother, but something more than an inkling of them has reached the consciousness of the elder daughter Cathleen. When Maurya moans:

> "Isn't it a hard and cruel man won't hear a word from an old woman, and she holding him from the sea?",

Cathleen answers:

> "It's the life of a young man to be going on the sea . . ."

---

[3] Susanne K. Langer, *Philosophy in a New Key: A Study in the Symbolism of Reason, Rite, and Art* (Cambridge, Mass. and London, 1951), p. 288.
[4] Kenneth Burke, "Thanatopsis for Critics: A Brief Thesaurus of Deaths and Dying," *Essays in Criticism*, II, 4 (October, 1952), 370.

What we have here is at least the beginning of a sense of values (not material or self-preservative, but moral) which owes nothing to the normal regard for survival.

A significant factor in the play is the continuous preoccupation over a period of nine days with finding and seeing Michael's body, the desire to know the score in the cruel game between the Sea and Maurya. The identification of Michael's body is a further victory for the Sea and prepares the way for the last victory of all, Bartley: the final destruction is now inevitable: no creative principle can be left.

Of the means by which Synge has presented dramatically his vision of "the whole external despondency of the clouds and sea",[5] the most significant is his insistence on the foolproof continuity of Death or the Sea, on the one hand, and the broken, static remnants of the family, on the other. Except for the brief appearance of Bartley, the play presents existence in terms of female characters only: the creativity of the family is broken, only the women are left. Maurya sees in the departure of Bartley the last piece of stability, of continuity, gone:

> "If it was a hundred horses, or a thousand horses, you had itself, what is the price of a thousand horses against a son where there is one son only?"

On the other hand, the nature of Death is presented in the idea of repetition, of continuity. Maurya, telling of the drowning of the other members of her family, says:

> "I was sitting here with Bartley, and he a baby lying on my two knees, and I seen two women, and three women, and four women coming in, and they crossing themselves and not saying a word. I looked out then, and there were men coming after them, and they holding a thing in the half of a red sail, and water dripping out of it—it was a dry day, Nora—and leaving a track to the door." /56/

The same words are repeated almost immediately by Nora, the next generation, when she looks out of the window and sees the women approaching:

> "They're carrying a thing among them, and there's water dripping out of it and leaving a track by the big stones."

The track of water in these situations becomes a symbol of the way by which Death comes, from the sea straight to the house, to the family.

---

[5] *The Aran Islands*, p. 91.

The implications of the play are intensified also by some important word-patterns. For instance, when Bartley has gone off, Cathleen cries out:

"The Son of God forgive us, Nora, we're after forgetting his bit of bread",

and Nora answers:

"And its destroyed he'll be going till dark night, and he after eating nothing since the sun went up."

Cathleen repeats the word:

"It's destroyed he'll be, surely . . .",

and from here on, the simple idea of hunger takes on the deeper over-tones of real destruction, gathering these implications until the word is used at last by Cathleen in this sense alone:

"It's destroyed we are from this day. It's destroyed, surely."

It is important to remember that "Riders to the Sea" has very little "incident", and little "character-development": Maurya is not indi-vidualized, except to the extent that she lives in a particular place. Rather, she is the Mother, the pathetic custodian of the family-unit. Within her dramatic existence she represents the tragedy (we may so describe it for the moment) of a human being whose life is condi-tioned by a grotesquely unequal conflict with a huge, destructive, natural force. She is deliberately presented as such: more than a human being, she is a symbol in ritual, and "Riders to the Sea" exploits the dramatic tensions which arise from the close contact of ritual and realism. "These people make no distinction between the natural and the supernatural."[6]

I have referred to the play as a "tragedy" and V. S. Pritchett goes much further in describing it as "genuinely tragic tragedy"[7]: but it seems to me necessary immediately to limit and define the term in this context. "Riders to the Sea" is not built on the "classic" lines of tragedy, in which (as, for instance, in "Oedipus Rex") the hero (or, if you prefer, the soul) moves from "purpose" (the taking of a step, an attitude) through action or passion (the pain arising from action) to final perception, a new awareness. "Riders to the Sea" does not follow

---

[6] *The Aran Islands*, p. 109.

[7] V. S. Pritchett, "The End of the Gael," *In My Good Books* (London, 1943), p. 158.

this pattern: at any stage, the taking by Maurya of a positive course of action is impossible because the scales are too heavily weighted against her (a human conflict is one thing, but conflict between an old woman and the Sea is another). For this reason, /57/ action is frustrated, purpose cannot even be formulated. The play ends in Maurya's Acceptance, rather than in any positive perception. But it is necessary to carry the argument somewhat further.

The "plot" of "Riders to the Sea" and the fact that it is capable of being described by no convenient alternative word to "tragedy" makes it necessary to clarify our conception of the tragic experience. We may gladly avail ourselves of a modern description of that experience: "The sense of heightened life that goes with the tragic experience is conditioned by a transcending of the ego—an escape from all attitudes of self-assertion . . . the experience is constructive or creative, and involves a recognizing positive value as in some way defined and vindicated by death. It is as if we were challenged at the profoundest level with the question, 'In what does the significance of life reside?', and found ourselves contemplating, for answer, a view of life, and of the things giving it value, that makes the valued appear unquestionably more important than the valuer, so that significance lies, clearly and inescapably, in the willing adhesion of the individual self to something other than itself."[8] It seems to me that this formulation is just: and on this basis "Riders to the Sea" does not constitute the tragic experience, for at least three reasons: firstly, because Maurya's Acceptance which ends the play has in it nothing of the positive "willing adhesion of the individual self to something other than itself": secondly, because there is in the play no significant equivalent of "the valued", and thirdly, because in the final analysis the play does not give "the sense of heightened life". We may even add a fourth reason, that Maurya's sufferings are determined by forces which do not include her will or her character.

The precise beginning of Acceptance for Maurya is significantly the moment at which Bartley, the last of her sons, is brought in drowned. In her next speech, it is seen that Bartley's death comes as a relief to her: as long as any one of her sons remained, the Sea would continue its destruction: now, all that is finished, and Maurya says:

"They're all gone now, and there isn't anything more the sea can do to me. . . . I'll have no call now to be up crying and praying when the wind breaks from the south, and you can hear the surf is in the east,

---

8 F. R. Leavis, "Tragedy and the 'Medium' ", *The Common Pursuit* (London, 1952), pp. 131-132.

and the surf is in the west, making a great stir with the two noises, and they hitting one on the other. I'll have no call now to be going down and getting Holy Water in the dark nights after Samhain, and I won't care what way the sea is when the other women will be keening."

The fact of poverty will remain, but there will be rest and sleep, ease to the mind: /58/

"It's a great rest I'll have now, and great sleeping in the long nights after Samhain, if it's only a bit of wet flour we do have to eat, and maybe a fish that would be stinking."

"Riders to the Sea" is not a tragedy: to see the play is to feel a pathetic rather than a tragic experience. But if the intensity of the feeling which it arouses blurs the distinction between pathos and tragedy, it is because Synge has attained contact with and exploited dramatically that area in the human subconscious which fears the "other" forces, thunder, darkness, lightning, earthquake and ocean. For this reason, the sea becomes far more than a mere setting for "Riders to the Sea" and takes on the significance of the forest in "The Emperor Jones" or the mill-race in "Rosmersholm", the silent, inhuman agent which reveals weaknesses, destroys all human defences and finally sums up the story in death.

Jan Setterquist

*Riders to the Sea, The Lady from the Sea, Rosmersholm**

At about the time he wrote *In the Shadow of the Glen* Synge was writing another one-act play, *Riders to the Sea,* first performed in 1904.

The action of this play takes place on a small island off the west coast of Ireland. The plot is extremely plain and may be told in a few words.

The central figure of the drama is the old fisherman's widow, Maurya, the mother of six sons. Only the youngest, Bartley, is left to her. The sea has taken the others, as it took her husband. Bartley is now preparing to ride to the sea-shore on his way to a horse-fair on the mainland. The old woman, feeling the approach of disaster, tries in vain to persuade her son to stay at home. But Bartley refuses to be prevailed upon. He sets out, without his mother's blessing, on his red mare for the ride which Maurya with the audience is convinced will be his last. Shortly afterwards Bartley's sisters discover that they have completely forgotten to give him any food for the journey. Now his mother feels she must intercept her son and give him her bread and her blessing.

As soon as the old woman has gone, the two daughters begin to examine a bundle of clothes belonging to an islander who has been

* Reprinted from Jan Setterquist, *Ibsen and the Beginnings of Anglo-Irish Drama, I. John Millington Synge,* being Volume 2 of *Upsala Irish Studies,* edited by S. B. Liljegren. Upsala: A. -B. Lundequistka Bokhandeln, 1951, pp. 27-39. Reprinted by permission of the author and the editor.

found drowned. At the opening of the play they had been looking at the clothes, but had hidden them from their mother, fearing they might have belonged to their lost brother, Michael. A further examination shows their worst fears to be justified. The sea has taken Michael as its prey. /28/

At that moment Maurya returns, looking haggard and forlorn. She still carries the little parcel of food. Disregarding her daughters, she begins singing mournfully to herself. Asked if she has seen Bartley, she gives the evasive reply: "My heart's broken from this day." She then tells them that she has seen a most dreadful sight. Bartley was riding his red mare. After him came his grey pony. But its rider was now his brother Michael, dressed in his best clothes and with fine new shoes on his feet. The mother tried to speak, but could not utter a word. All of a sudden the frightful meaning of the vision was brought home to her. It was a portent. The sea was on the point of taking Bartley from her, too, as it had already taken her husband and her other sons. She remembers how under identical circumstances she lost her son Patch. She has scarcely finished telling her daughters of the tragedy, when several women enter the cottage. They make the sign of the cross and kneel down with their red skirts drawn over their heads as a sign of deep mourning. Maurya, feeling their presence rather than actually seeing them, asks dreamily if they are grieving for Patch or for Michael. She can no longer be kept in ignorance. They tell her that Michael has been found dead and laid to rest in the north of the island. The women have gathered in her house to wait for Bartley. His dead body is then brought into the cottage, wrapped in a bit of a sail which leaves a trail of sea-water on the floor. All, except Maurya, kneel at his bier, and the women begin to keen. But Maurya does not heed them. Her lifelong struggle with the forces of Nature has come to an end. She is beyond the reach of any earthly sorrow. "They are all gone now, and there isn't anything more the sea can do to me . . ." The old mother bends her head in resignation: "No man at all can be living for ever, and we must be satisfied." Thus ends this tragedy of a whole family beaten in their unequal struggle against the cruelty of an implacable sea.

As will be seen from the summary above, none of the characters in the play, not even the mother, has the central rôle in *Riders to the Sea*. For the sea itself, which Synge apparently regards as a symbol of Death, rules the lives of the islanders and controls their destinies. It is their sworn enemy; and yet also their perfidious ally. /29/ For these people draw their sustenance from its depths. To the older generation who know the Atlantic in all its moods, and especially to the mothers, symbolized by old Maurya, it is the source of terror and woe and sleepless anxiety for those they love. But to the young people it is a lure and an enticement; its call makes them insensible to the warnings of their elders. Old Maurya sees with a heavy heart how her son leaves his home for certain death. "He's gone now, God spare us, and we'll not see him again. He's gone now, and when the black night is falling I'll have no son left me in the world."[1] The youthful confidence of her daughter offers an effective contrast to the old woman's complaint: "It's the life of a young man to be going on the sea, and who would listen to an old woman with one thing and she saying it over."[2]

Life—and death, that is the sea as reflected in the minds of two generations. The sea, which at the same time frightens and allures, repels and attracts its victims, is the very key-note of the play, and may be regarded as its catalyst. Unchangeable and invisible to the audience, the sea plays a fateful part in the drama, inexorably hastening the catastrophe which is foretold from the beginning.

If this introductory analysis of *Riders to the Sea* is placed as a basis for the scrutiny of Ibsen, it becomes obvious that his work during the 1880's includes two dramas which show several points of approach to that play. One of them attracts attention by its very title, namely *The Lady from the Sea* (1888). Because, in this drama, too, the sea may be said to play the principal part.

As has already been pointed out, the pivot of the plot is a discordant marriage. The wife, in her girlhood, was attracted to a man who like herself felt that he belonged to the sea, and she had never been able to muster up strength to rid herself of his influence.

In Ibsen's play, as in Synge's, the attraction of the sea is felt as a hidden undercurrent throughout the drama. Halvdan Koht, who is, perhaps, the greatest living authority on Ibsen, very rightly points out that in this drama the sea became both a spiritual power and a symbol. It represented, he adds, the attraction of the unknown—and, perhaps, of the primitive in man himself.[3] /30/

Those who consciously deny the call of the sea, forfeit their peace of mind. Life on shore must of necessity seem incomplete to those whose affinities are with the sea. So it appears to Ibsen's heroine,

---

[1] *Riders to the Sea*, p. 37.
[2] *Ibid.*, p. 37.
[3] Halvdan Koht, *Henrik Ibsen*, I–II (Oslo 1928--29), vol. II, p. 281.

Ellida Wangel. The fateful events of her youth have marked her for life. She is enthralled by "the Stranger" who symbolizes the sea, even in details such as the pearl of the pin, in his tie, as that pearl resembles the eye of a fish. As early as the first act, one of Ellida's girlhood friends gives vent to the following opinion about her: "I should rather say that you, Mrs. Wangel, stand in a peculiar relation to the sea and all that belongs to it." And Ellida answers: "Well, you may be right. I almost think so myself."[4] Her real feelings, however, are no doubt most clearly displayed in a long conversation with her husband, Dr. Wangel. "Night and day," she says, "winter and summer, it is upon me this haunting home-sickness for the sea."[5] When her husband in the kindness of his heart proposes to take Ellida out to "the salt-laden, sweeping sea-breezes" in order to cure her of her obsession, she cries out hysterically:

> ELLIDA. Oh, don't speak of it! Don't think of such a thing! There is no help for me in that! I know, I feel, that I should not be able to throw it off out there either.
> WANGEL. To throw what off, dear? What do you mean?
> ELLIDA. I mean the terror of him. His unfathomable power over my soul—[6]

Towards the end of the drama there is a significant hint of the horror of the sea in the following dialogue:

> WANGEL (*nearer*). Tell me, Ellida—what do you really mean by "terrible"?
> ELLIDA (*reflects*). I call a thing terrible—when it both frightens and fascinates me.
> WANGEL. Fascinates?
> ELLIDA. Most of all when it fascinates me—I think.
> WANGEL (*slowly*). You are akin to the sea.
> ELLIDA. There is terror in that too.[7] /31/
> WANGEL. And in yourself no less.[8] You both frighten and fascinate.[9]

The third act largely consists of a synthesis of Ellida's "philosophy of the sea"[10] and it ends with the following conversation, which offers

---

[4] *The Lady from the Sea*, Act I (C. W., IX, p. 187).
[5] *Ibid.*, Act II, p. 223.
[6] *Ibid.*, Act II, p. 235. (Lit. "I mean 'the terrible'; this incomprehensible power over the mind.")
[7] Lit. "So is the horror" ('the terrible'.)
[8] Lit. "And the horror ('the terrible') in its turn is akin to you."
[9] *The Lady from the Sea*, Act IV, pp. 306-307.
[10] *Ibid.*, Act III, pp. 253-255 and *passim*.

a brilliant and comprehensive explanation of the lure "the Stranger" has for her:

> ELLIDA (*softly and trembling*). Oh Wangel—save me from myself.
> WANGEL (*looks anxiously at her*). Ellida! I feel it—there is something behind all this.
> ELLIDA. All that allures is behind it.
> WANGEL. All that allures—?
> ELLIDA. That man is like the sea.[11]

In the *dénouement* of the last act Ellida succeeds in attaining spiritual freedom only after a terrible inner struggle:

> ELLIDA (*with an outburst of emotion*). Oh—what is it that tempts and allures and seems to drag me into the unknown! The whole might of the sea is centred in this one thing![12]

Finally, when the transformation has taken place, Wangel says:

> ELLIDA—your mind is like the sea: it has its ebb and flow.[13]

The sea and the attraction it exerts is not, however, the only element in *Riders to the Sea* reminiscent of Ibsen. As will appear from the above summary of the plot, there is a scene in which old Maurya tells her daughters of a vision she had. Her two sons, one of whom had already been drowned, appeared to her, astride their horses. The sight of the "Riders to the Sea" fills the old woman with horror. At once she knows for certain that she will never see her sons alive again. Shortly afterwards there is the news of Bartley's and Michael's fate. Of the former the narrative runs: "The /32/ grey pony knocked him over into the sea, and he was washed out where there is a great surf on the white rocks."[14]

The suggestive vision of the horses and its interpretation as a portent of death is reminiscent of Ibsen's *Rosmersholm*, published in 1886. It so happens that there, too, visions, signs and portents play a considerable part. The "ghosts of the manor" are two horses which appear whenever someone of the family is going to die. Indeed this theme is so closely interwoven with the play that Ibsen originally intended to call it *White Horses* instead of *Rosmersholm*.[15]

---

[11] *Ibid.*, Act III, pp. 272–273.
[12] *Ibid.*, Act V, p. 341.
[13] *Ibid.*, Act V, p. 345. About 50 other allusions to the sea and its powerful influence upon man are to be found in *The Lady from the Sea*. As, however, they add little or nothing to the argument, the above quotations will suffice.
[14] *Riders to the Sea*, p. 48.
[15] Koht, *op. cit.*, vol. II, p. 266.

The constant occurrence of symbols is a characteristic feature of Ibsen's work during the 1880's. They introduce an element of ambiguity into his plays during that period. With certain modifications this may also be said to be the case with Synge's first plays.

It has already been shown above that Synge uses the *motif* of the horses to presage the catastrophe. Likewise in *Rosmersholm* the heroine "in broad daylight" catches a glimpse of the white horses of the manor and feels them to be portents of impending doom.[16] "The white horses," Tennant says, "which haunt *Rosmersholm* help to give the suicide of Rosmer and Rebekka in the fatal mill-race an illusion of inevitability."[17] Thus they may also be said to exercise a certain influence upon the technique of the play.

Similarly, *Riders to the Sea*, is instinct with the same atmosphere of inevitability. This applies not only to the vision described above, but more particularly to the indomitable natural forces which are at work in the two plays. In both *Riders to the Sea* and *The Lady from the Sea* it has already been observed that an irresistible attraction is inherent in the sea. In *Rosmersholm* there is furthermore the mill-race which inexorably takes as its prey first one, then another member of the family, exactly as the sea does in *Riders to the Sea*. Koht is quite right in pointing out that there is one thing in particular in *Rosmersholm* that singles out this play from Ibsen's older works, *viz.* the power exerted by Nature over the human mind.[18] /33/

The previous history of the characters in Ibsen's drama is as follows: The hero, Johannes Rosmer, is an idealist of the noblest type whose marriage is childless. His wife, however, although a noble woman, has not the mind best suited to helping him in his struggle to put into practice his utopian dreams of a community of noble souls. A young woman, Rebekka West, comes to Rosmersholm and by subtle suggestions she deliberately induces Rosmer's wife to believe that she is the real obstacle preventing her husband from fulfilling his mission. Finally Rebekka achieves her aim. Mrs. Rosmer, in a fit of desperation, throws herself into the mill-race and the new lady of the house takes her place as Rosmer's partner. Towards the end of the drama the master of Rosmersholm discovers that it was Rebekka, the woman he has ended by loving and trusting, who harried his wife to her death. And then he feels that he is no less guilty than she, and that only by voluntarily throwing themselves into the mill-race can they atone for their crime.

---

[16] *Rosmersholm*, Act III (C. W., IX, p. 133).
[17] Tennant, *op. cit.*, p. 115.
[18] Koht, *op. cit.*, vol. II, p. 273.

Thus the fatal mill-stream, which is never seen, but the roar of whose waters is heard in the distance throughout the play, gradually acquires the grandeur of a natural force which irresistibly sucks down the people of Rosmersholm, exactly as the sea does with the characters in *Riders to the Sea.*

Here, the objection may, of course, be raised that Synge might easily have found both the theme of the inexorable forces of Nature and the fatal vision of the horses in the storehouse of his island experience. As a matter of fact there is definite proof of his having done so in the latter case. Synge himself relates a little episode in his travel-sketches *The Aran Islands* which also seems to explain his choice of the rather peculiar title *Riders to the Sea.* The story, which is to be found at the end of the book, tells us how a young man was drowned on his way to the southernmost island. It is narrated in the following words:

> "Before he went out on the sea that day his dog came up and sat beside him on the rocks, and began crying. When the horses were coming down to the slip an old woman saw her son, that was drowned a while ago, riding on one of them. She didn't say what she was after seeing, and this man caught the horse, he caught his own horse /34/ first, and then he caught this one, and after that he went out and was drowned."[19]

This, however, does not necessarily exclude a possible reminiscence of Ibsen. For the Aran book is full of such striking incidents which Synge, perhaps in part for lack of time—he began writing late and died comparatively young—but probably also for various other reasons, never put into use for a drama. Yet many of them would appear to be extremely suitable for dramatic purposes. It may suffice here to mention only the pathetic scene of a woman being evicted from her home: "The outrage to a tomb in China probably gives no greater shock to the Chinese than the outrage to a hearth in Inishmaan gives to the people," says Synge laconically.[20]

Here, as elsewhere, it may be presumed that the episode of the horses and, indeed, the whole of the evocative description of the sea, acquired additional dramatic significance for Synge when he saw the highly effective use to which Ibsen put similar themes in *Rosmersholm* and *The Lady from the Sea.*

The vision of the horses was, as has already been indicated, partly a technical device. It may, perhaps, be considered appropriate at this point to add a few remarks about the technique of *Riders to the Sea.*

---

[19] John Millington Synge, *The Aran Islands* (Dublin 1912), p. 222.
[20] Synge, *op. cit.,* p. 78.

Synge has been justly praised for his ability to evoke, with great
economy of means, a vivid impression of the proximity and power of
the sea. One of his biographers (Corkery) makes the following interesting observation:

"Synge makes the old woman, mother of many fishermen, never refer
to the sea except as—the sea. Her phrases are: the sea; on the sea; in
the sea; by the sea. There is never an adjective; no personification; no
synonym. The word ocean does not occur. Yet how terribly aware of the
malice of the sea we become!"[21]

On the whole, this passage could—*mutatis mutandis*—be applied
to *The Lady from the Sea*. There is hardly a single qualifying ad- /35/
jective to be found in Ibsen's masterly hinting at the all-pervading
presence of the sea during the entire five acts of this play. Ellida
herself says simply "the sea," "on the sea," "in the sea," "over the
sea," "of the sea," "from the sea," and "to the sea."[22]
Furthermore, the sea is perceived from the stage in neither of the
two plays. Ibsen says definitely in one of his stage-directions: "The
open sea is not visible."[23] Primarily this may no doubt be regarded as
a concession to technical difficulties. On the other hand, it is con-
ceivable that both Ibsen and Synge were fully aware of the fact that
the mere mention of the sea and its power over man was likely to
make an even stronger impression on the audience than if it were
actually represented as part of the scenery. The same calculation
almost certainly accounts for the treatment of the mill-race in
Rosmersholm. The emotional effect of the fatal stream is the greater
because it remains invisible, the strange sound of its rushing waters
being only heard in the distance throughout the action of the play.
The contrast between the small, dark cottage and the unseen ocean
outside it is quite in keeping with the "Ibsen tradition." Indeed, it
was a literary fashion for quite a long time to criticize Ibsen for the
stuffy atmosphere of his plays with their frequent indoor settings.
Somewhat premature conclusions as regards Ibsen's attitude towards
Nature were readily drawn from the fact that, with the passing of the
years, he became less and less inclined to stir from his own hearth.
But even a cursory reading of his stage-instructions reveals the fact
that, especially in his later works, he was particularly fond of *outdoor*
settings for his plays, such as a mountainous or a coastal landscape.[24]

---

[21] Daniel Corkery, *Synge and Anglo-Irish Literature* (Oxford 1947), pp. 140–141.
[22] *The Lady from the Sea, passim.*
[23] *Ibid.*, stage-direction for act II.
[24] See *e.g. Brand, Peer Gynt, The Lady from the Sea, Little Eyolf, John Gabriel
Borkman,* and *When We Dead Awaken.*

And he retained his fondness for the sea throughout his life. Even in this respect Ibsen's stage-directions are, indeed, most illuminating.

In his delineation of "the Stranger," however, Ibsen used a kind of "sea-symbolism" never found in the works of Synge. Here it will suffice to recall Ellida's remark: "That man is like the sea."[25] /36/ On the other hand, the previous study has clearly shown Synge to have been perfectly familiar with the use of the symbol as a literary means of expression.[26] In Riders to the Sea the old Aran fisherwife grows in stature as her sorrows increase throughout the action of the play, until at the end she is represented as a symbol of all the islanders and their tenacious, unequal struggle against the irresistible forces of Nature.

It is, perhaps, the strong feeling of Destiny pervading Riders to the Sea which has led many critics to compare it to the classical drama. Corkery, for instance, says: "The greatness of Riders to the Sea lies in this: that it is one of the few modern plays written, and successfully written, in the Greek genre."[27] Lamm (one of the few Swedes who has written about Synge) says in his book on modern drama that there is probably no other contemporary play which, without the slightest deviation from naturalistic technique, conveys so much of the classical atmosphere, with its all-enveloping sense of doom.[28] This is almost equally true of Ibsen's later works which include an impressive number of tragedies of Destiny. They differ, however, from Synge's dramas in one particular respect, namely that either the hero or the heroine sinks beneath the weight of a "tragic guilt" rooted in the past. Sometimes they perish together.

But it is not an indispensable condition of Greek drama that disaster should arise from past misdeeds. A well-known Swedish scholar (Schück) points out that, in a Greek tragedy, the fall of the hero may be due to a defect of character—the impetuous Ajax is a case in point—but this is certainly not necessary, and the poet does not emphasize it in any way. Œdipus is irritable and hot-tempered, but his misfortunes are not caused by these defects; they are predestined, like those of Antigone.[29] This might also be said of Bartley in Riders to the Sea who certainly does not meet with disaster because he has defied his mother. Thus the flavour of an- /37/ tiquity, with

---

[25] The Lady from the Sea, Act III, p. 273.
[26] See above, p. 21.
[27] Corkery, op. cit., p. 108.
[28] Lamm, op. cit., pp. 311–312.
[29] Henrik Schück, Illustrerad allmän litteraturhistoria, vol. I, (Stockholm 1919), pp. 137–138.

the theme of Destiny strongly accentuated, is found in both Synge and Ibsen.

There are also several technical peculiarities in *Riders to the Sea* reminiscent of the Ibsenian drama. This is evident in Synge's method of increasing the tension by causing the action to be interrupted as soon as something important is about to be revealed, such as the identity of the owner of the clothes in *Riders to the Sea*, or, in Ibsen's case, the name of "the Stranger" in *The Lady from the Sea.*

Devices of this kind are, of course, common to all dramatists. But they may be adduced as proofs in the case of Synge because his work shows several other technical characteristics usually regarded as peculiar to the Ibsen drama. One is to be found in the extraordinarily clever way in which Ibsen, by the use of parallel scenes, manages to evoke the past. We have already found how he applied this technique in a striking way in *Rosmersholm,* where the final tragedy in the mill-stream is, as it were, a terrible repetition of a suicide which took place before the opening of the drama. Among numerous other instances there is, however, one of particular interest in this connection, namely the last scene of the first act of *Ghosts* (1881). Regina's cry: "Oswald! take care! are you mad? Let me go!" is heard from the next room, immediately after Mrs. Alving has been telling the Reverend Manders how she once caught her own husband and the housemaid in exactly the same situation.[30]

This "ghost scene" has been duly praised. Consequently, it is interesting to notice how Synge uses precisely the same technique in *Riders to the Sea.* In the scene in which old Maurya tells her daughters how, long ago, the sea gave her back one of her dead sons, she says:

> "I was sitting here with Bartley, and he a baby lying on my two knees, and I seen two women, and three women, and four women coming in, and they crossing themselves and not saying a word. I looked out then, and there were men coming after them, and they holding a thing in the half of a red sail, and water dripping out of it—it was a dry day, Nora—and leaving a track to the door."[31] /38/

The old woman has hardly finished her vivid description of how one of her drowned sons was brought home, when the shadow of the past begins to haunt the scene as Bartley's home-coming mirrors that of his brother down to the smallest particular.

---

[30] *Ghosts,* Act I (C. W., VII, p. 213),
[31] *Riders to the Sea*, pp. 46–47.

Finally, some mention should perhaps be made of the manner in which Synge differs from Ibsen. In *Riders to the Sea* as in *In the Shadow of the Glen* the differences are primarily due to the fact that the milieu described by Synge, and, consequently, the social position of his chief characters, are so utterly unlike those we find in the works of Ibsen. The people whom the Irish playwright depicts are all inhabitants of the Aran Islands, a group of isolated rocky islands some way out in the Atlantic. In this community, certainly one of the most primitive to be found in Europe, Synge himself lived among the fishermen as one of themselves, sharing their simple fare. He felt instinctively akin to the islanders with their primitive, sometimes almost savage gaiety, which nothing, not even the insatiable sea, is likely to subdue.

Scenes such as the keening of the old people, the herding of cattle, or the arrest of a wrongdoer by the local police, accompanied by vociferous oaths, were almost daily events which had a stimulating effect upon Synge's creative imagination, already highly-developed. A closer study of his plays reveals very clearly to what an extent their construction depends on personal experiences and impressions of such scenes; invaluable sources of inspiration for a responsive artist.

Furthermore, Synge deliberately refrains from drawing any kind of moral conclusions. It is typical of him that he shows no interest whatever in the question as to whether Bartley ought or ought not to have obeyed his mother. As in *In the Shadow of the Glen*, it is for the audience, or the reader, to form an opinion as to the solution of the problem. Thus, once again, we are unmistakably reminded of Ibsen who was accustomed to dispose of importunate questions with the retort: "I prefer to ask, it is not my task to answer."

On the other hand, *Riders to the Sea*, unlike its immediate predecessor, might almost be looked upon as being a play with a purpose. For it is difficult not to feel that, in creating the figure of /39/ Maurya, Synge consciously or unconsciously paid tribute to the hardy fisherfolk, whose joys and sorrows he had made his own, eating their bread and salt and sharing their vigils.

Taken separately it is true that none of the above-mentioned similarities can be said to justify a definite conclusion as to the extent of Ibsen's influence on Synge. However, it is equally true that, placed together, the various parallels drawn above form a body of evidence supporting the theory that the connexion between Synge and his Norwegian predecessor, though hitherto unjustifiably disregarded, is far from negligible.

Alan Price

Riders to the Sea*

Riders to the Sea is probably one of the shortest and most concise plays in the language. In it a number of Synge's diverse experiences, along with the predominant interests and attitudes of his life and writings, are fused into a new whole, which sets forth the essence of Aran life and which is also Synge's image of Man's place in the universe.

I find difficulty in following the criticism voiced by D. Figgis[1] that the play lacks progression, is a stasis, that it is 'a slice of life set in the atmosphere of tragedy. Even as there is not water in a mist of the hills because it is all moisture, so there is not tragedy in *Riders to the Sea* because it is all tragical.' Clearly, the tragedy is centred on the figure of Maurya; she is the true tragic protagonist, and the rest of the figures have only varying degrees of partial awareness of the meaning of the whole. They have not yet attained her tragic stature and insight, nor reached that final illumination which sees life as essentially tragic, and, accepting this fact, gains thereby 'calm of mind all passion spent'. Furthermore, there are in this play both progression and also variety and contrast of texture, pace and mood. The play can be seen to fall into four movements: (*a*) (pp. 37–39½)[2] the exposition; mood —near normal, subdued, apprehensive; method—mainly naturalistic and the particular; (*b*) (pp. 39½–42) the development; mood—more elevated, antiphony between Maurya and Bartley; method—mainly symbolic, suggesting the universal through the particular; (*c*) (pp. 43–7) a variation; mood—domestic pathos; method—mainly natural-

---

* Reprinted from *Synge and Anglo-Irish Drama*. London: Metheun, 1961, pp. 181-91, by permission of the publisher. © 1961 by Alan Price.

[1] *Studies and Appreciations* (London, 1912), p. 42.
[2] *Plays* (London, 1932). All page numbers in brackets refer to this edition.

istic and the particular, rising to (*d*) (pp. 48–end) the climax and
resolution—the lament and benediction by Maurya in which the
universal shines through the particular. These movements are parts
of a seamless whole, and the increase or decrease of tension and
significance is always the logical outcome of the circumstances. /182/

(*a*) The play opens on a level near enough to the everyday world
to persuade an audience to accept it without difficulty as a valid
representation of life. The young girl, Cathleen, who deftly kneads
the cake, puts it into the oven and at once begins to spin at the wheel
(so hard is existence that she cannot pause for a minute), is reassur-
ingly life-like. And the quiet entry of the younger sister, Nora, carrying the bundle, together with their simple words, completes and
establishes the dramatic illusion. Their restrained tones and movements, Cathleen's sudden action of stopping the wheel and listening
when Michael's name is mentioned, and the way they are startled
when the door is suddenly blown open, all indicate plainly the strain
and anxiety under which they labour. This is threefold: anxiety lest
Maurya should hear about the bundle; anxiety lest it confirm the
death of Michael; anxiety about Bartley's proposed journey. Thus the
scene is set, essential information is put over economically and naturally, foreboding is aroused by the sight of the new boards, and the
recurrent references to the rampant sea, and curiosity stimulated
regarding the contents of the bundle, hidden unopened in the turf-loft,
before Maurya enters.

(*b*) Worry is ravaging Maurya; as is shown by her querulousness,
and by the way she repeats her sayings, groping for comfort; 'He
won't go this day with the wind rising from the south and west. He
won't go this day, for the young priest will stop him surely' (39).
Young Nora, unthinking, tells her mother that the priest cannot stop
Bartley and he is bent on going; and Maurya braces herself for a final
struggle to keep back her last son from the sea. The rest of this movement is a battle of wills, with the mother trying desperately to break
her son's resolve to carry on the ageless tradition of their kind, of
wresting a living from the sea; a battle the more tense because it
cannot be fought openly and directly but is carried on by nuance and
suggestion—Cathleen and Nora are hardly aware that it is happening.
Bartley, sad and quiet, is already a doomed man; his sisters cannot
see this yet (when they are older and mothers they may), but Bartley
knows it, and so does Maurya. But she cannot express this premoni-
tion directly; if she did Bartley would be bound to scoff at it as a
mere fancy and be more determined to go. Maurya, in fact, is
severely handicapped in this crucial struggle. If she describes the
dangers of the journey fully, she will distress the girls further, per-

haps /183/ unnecessarily, and she may provoke Bartley into going in order to show that she is wrong and that he is not a coward, particularly as other men are attempting the trip, and the priest has not forbidden it. At the same time the nature of the people (their self-respect and reserve) and their traditions prevent her both from begging or ordering him not to go. And so she catches at his every word and gesture, trying to wring from them some reason why he should stay. This gives a kind of versicle and response quality to the speech which is peculiarly elevated and potent, making an incantation or ritual for approaching death, and seeming symbolical of thousands of similar scenes. Pathos is further heightened by the way Bartley ignores his mother, and gives directions to the girls regarding the tasks to be done about the home, as if his absence was only to be temporary, though it is clear to an audience that he is really departing for ever. When Bartley takes the rope Maurya tells him to leave it because it will be needed to bury Michael, but he replies: 'I've no halter the way I can ride down on the mare, and I must go now quickly. This is the one boat going for two weeks or beyond it, and the fair will be a good fair for horses, I heard them saying below' (40). She snatches, as is her custom, at his last words: 'It's a hard thing they'll be saying below if the body is washed up and there's no man in it to make the coffin, and I after giving a big price for the finest boards you'd find in Connemara' (41). Like most primitive peoples these islanders are sticklers for custom and social proprieties, and she stresses the importance of observing due form, in the hope that this will make him stay: although her real worry is not that Michael, if washed up, will not get a decent burial, but that Bartley will go to sea. Bartley resists her, and her tone intensifies to a searching question: 'If it was a hundred horses, or a thousand horses, you had itself, what is the price of a thousand horses against a son where there is one son only?' (41). This cry, addressed to Bartley, also reverberates through our minds; it is a prayer for a true sense of values, a refusal to weigh one human life in the same scales as commercial gain, and a protest against conditions of life which compel men to risk their lives constantly in order to gain a bare subsistence. Is life worth having on such terms? It is a question which echoes through the play; but Bartley dare not consider the question, let alone attempt to answer it, and he goes on giving directions to the girls, ending: 'It's hard /184/ set we'll be from this day with no one in it but one man to work.' Once more Maurya pounces on his words, desperate now that she is losing the struggle, and dropping all reserve, forced to make the direct appeal: 'It's hard set we'll be surely the day you're drowned with the rest. What way will I live and the girls with me, and I an old woman looking for the grave?' (42). At this tense moment there is a stage direction: '(*Bartley lays down halter, takes off his old coat, and puts on a newer one of the same flannel.*)' Bartley in performing these simple movements in silence—while the girls look on doubtfully and Maurya yearns towards him in agony—shows that he is deeply moved by his mother's appeal and distress and is almost persuaded not to go. At last this extremely effective moment of stillness, seeming so long, is ended as Bartley makes some slight gesture indicating decision. Then he asks about the boat and says, with great tragic irony, 'I'll be coming again in two days.' Maurya knows she is defeated and breaks into lament: 'Isn't it a hard and cruel man won't hear a word from an old woman, and she holding him from the sea?' (42). Cathleen's quick reply to this expresses an attitude completely opposed to Maurya's: 'It's the life of a young man to be going on the sea, and who would listen to an old woman with one thing and she saying it over?' (42). Cathleen's words embody the outlook of those islanders who still have the hope that life may be bearable, even enjoyable; she is youth, courageously and confidently facing a life which the old woman, who has greater knowledge and experience, and who is shattered in spirit, now wishes to reject. Maurya's agony reaches a climax as Bartley departs: 'He is gone now, God spare us, and we'll not see him again. He's gone now, and when the black night is falling I'll have no son left me in the world' (43).

(*c*) But the time has not yet come (though it will) to stress and develop this theme. At this stage in the play some change of mood or pace, some variation of tension, are necessary, to give relief for highly charged emotions in both characters and audience, to forward the action and supply further essential information, particularly about the contents of the bundle, and to provide contrast with what has gone before and prepare for the ultimate climax. The transition from elevated and symbolic gesture and utterance to a concern with more domestic matters is brought about with great skill by Maurya's aimless raking at the fire (how /185/ natural and how expressive of her desolation this is) and by Cathleen's alarm about the cake:

> CATHLEEN: The Son of God forgive us, Nora, we're after forgetting his bit of bread.
> NORA: And it's destroyed he'll be going till dark night, and he after eating nothing since the sun went up (43).

At first sight their cries and their anxiety may appear to be excessive; why, when there is so much distress upon the house, should they make these outbursts about a mere matter of forgetting bread? But closer consideration will reveal how exact is Synge's understanding of psychology. The two girls *are* worried—about Michael and Bartley—but they cannot show their worry, they must put on a brave face for as long as they can; yet, at the same time, their pent-up feelings demand some outlet, and so this flaw in their domestic arrangements enables them to give vent to these feelings, without disclosing that they are really alarmed, not about the cake of bread, but about their brothers. Meanwhile Maurya, bowed over the turf fire, is visibly distressed, and the girls, partly in the hope that seeing Bartley again and giving him her blessing may console Maurya, and partly in order to get rid of her, advise Maurya to go out to the spring well. She goes out slowly and painfully, saying, with great pathos, as she takes Michael's stick: 'In the big world the old people do be leaving things after them for their sons and children, but in this place it is the young men do be leaving things behind for them that do be old.' They at once bring out the bundle, and Nora, in a few brief words that help to hold the play near to everyday actuality and suggest a normal world going on all round, tells how it was found: 'There were two men, and they rowing round with the poteen before the cocks crowed, and the oar of one of them caught the body and they passing the black cliffs of the north' (45). The two girls, like a person who has just received a message containing either very good or very bad news, are both eager and reluctant to open the bundle; yet anything is better than uncertainty, and they try to open it. But the tension is further intensified when the knot proves too tight and they have to find a knife and cut the string. By such simple means does Synge get his effects. Noteworthy too is the way Nora's youth and comparative inexperience of these crises are brought out by her artless questions: 'I've heard /186/ tell it was a long way to Donegal' and 'And what time would a man take, and he floating?' At such moments of intense stress and uncertainty the young person's mind, as if by some natural defence mechanism, swerves away into speculation. Most felicitous of all is the way in which the domestic and the tragic are mingled; ordinary things, such as the bundle, string and knot, the knife, the flannel shirt on the hook, acquire momentous meaning, and serve to set forth and heighten the tragic emotion. In addition, there can be few more sad experiences than handling the clothes of someone dear and lately dead, and it is by Nora's recognizing her dropped stitches that the truth is brought home. At once the language lifts from the quiet, anxious phrases they have been exchanging to a more passionate, unparticularized, lament:

> CATHLEEN: Ah, Nora, isn't it a bitter thing to think of him floating that way to the far north, and no-one to keen him but the black hags that do be flying on the sea?

NORA (*Swinging herself half round, and throwing out her arms on the
clothes.*) And isn't it a pitiful thing when there is nothing left of a
man who was a great rower and fisher but a bit of an old shirt and a
plain stocking? (46—7).

But they must go on living, and the immediate task is to prevent
Maurya knowing that Michael is drowned. Yet here too there is
pathos in the way in which the two girls have to devise subterfuges
to spare Maurya just a little sorrow and to allow her to retain her
hope about Michael for a few hours longer. In fact throughout the
play there is a general conspiracy for each person to hide, if not from
himself, at least from all the others, the terrible truth that death is
ever near and inexorable. Cathleen, though she is only twenty, is
already something of an expert in such evasions, and she tells Nora
to sit with her back to the light so that Maurya will not see that she
has been crying.

(*d*) But when Maurya enters she is not in a condition to remark
such features. She is absorbed by the vision of her dead husband and
sons she has just seen; and the rest of the play is one great lament by
Maurya for Bartley and Michael, for all her family, for all the islanders, for all men. In these few minutes Maurya goes through imagina-
tively a whole lifetime of suffering; seeing into the mystery of things
she finds at the core death, but, accepting this, she comes out on the
other side of grief with a kind of poise /187/ and calmness. This
lament is punctuated only by the brief words of Cathleen and the
islanders which serve to anchor the poetry and symbolism to normal-
ity, to blend the particular with the universal and to highlight the
tragic mood; how moving are the man's words on hearing that Maurya
has not thought of nails for the coffin: 'It's a great wonder she
wouldn't think of the nails, and all the coffin's she's seen made
already.' Cathleen, at this stage, is seen to be taking on all the responsibility for keeping the home together, now that her mother is
beyond it; she finds out how Bartley met his death, and arranges for
his burial, Maurya being no longer interested in such details, as she
becomes aware of something bigger, which includes and transcends
particularities.

In presenting this climax Synge uses the two fundamental methods
of the dramatist: narration and enactment on the stage, the classical
method and the modern. But the narration is not merely of a particular happening, it is of what has happened, is happening, and will
happen; just as the enactment is representative not of one event, but
of all. Maurya's narration evokes and concentrates a whole lifetime

of suffering and conflict; eight men move vividly across her imagination, and ours, all riders to the sea, which is death:

> I've had a husband, and a husband's father, and six sons in this house—
> six fine men, though it was a hard birth I had with every one of them
> and they coming to the world—and some of them were found and some
> of them were not found, but they're gone now the lot of them . . . (50).

The old woman's memory is better for far-off events, and it is while she is describing one of the earlier family disasters—how they brought the body in, the time Patch was drowned, when Bartley was only a baby on her knee—that the wheel comes full circle: they bring in the body of her last son. Her imagination has reduced multitude to unity, succession to an instant, her life has been made up seemingly of nothing but such scenes and she asks: 'Is it Patch or Michael, or what is it at all?' For her the sea seems almost saturated with dead men: 'There does be a power of young men floating round in the sea.' Here there is a particularly fine touch. Maurya is speaking, partly to Nora, as if to instruct and console her youngest child, and, with that knack many of us have of remembering trivial details in some moment of stress, she /188/ explains how they brought in Patch's body: 'A thing in the half of a red sail, and water dripping out of it—it was a dry day, Nora —and leaving a track to the door' (51). At this moment the islanders begin to enter, mourning, and Nora, looking out, sees the men carrying Bartley's body wrapped in a 'bit of red sail', and she cries: 'They're carrying a thing among them, and there's water dripping out of it and leaving a track by the big stones' (52). Nora is being initiated into this ritual of death. She is in the same position as her mother was many years ago; and in the future, it is implied, she will be in the position of Maurya, seeing her children brought home in this procession. It is always the same: in past, present, future, men ride down to the sea and are brought home in this way; nothing can break the cycle of 'these dying generations'.

The enactment on the stage too is the climax to Maurya's words, a concrete example to reinforce them, and also a symbolic representation of all the deaths on the island, and elsewhere. It hardly matters whether it is Patch or Michael or Bartley that is being brought home: all at some time or other find alike the inevitable end, and the one ritual we see on the stage is not only for Bartley but for all of them. Everything combines to persuade spectators that they are watching a scene of universal significance. There is no confusion, everyone knows what to do: the women enter ceremoniously, cross themselves, group

near the foot of the stage, and, putting their red petticoats over their
heads, begin to keen softly; the two girls quickly get the table out,
then kneel at the foot; the men place the body on the table with
practised ease, then take up their accustomed positions kneeling near
the door; and Maurya, like a priest taking his place at the altar, bows,
kneels by Bartley's head, and conducts the requiem.

Yet although Maurya uses Christian terms and symbols and sprinkles Bartley's body with Holy Water, she has come to a position
where, for her, the comforts of organized religion are of no avail.
The young priest had said that God would not leave her destitute with
no son living, but as Maurya declares, 'It's little the like of him knows
of the sea': she feels that the sea, the hunger for destruction at the
heart of the universe, is too powerful for the antidotes of religion.
Worn by repeated suffering and mourning, she has reached 'A condition of complete simplicity (Costing not less than everything)'; and
her gesture in putting the empty /189/ cup mouth downwards upon
Bartley's body symbolizes that she has drained life to the lees, and
feels that the end is come. Hence in her last great speeches it is not
so much on the agony she has experienced that she dwells but upon
the comfort that may come through total defeat and acquiescence;
she is getting beyond personal pain:

> They're all gone now, and there isn't anything more the sea can do
> to me . . . I'll have no call now to be up crying and praying when the
> wind breaks from the south, and you can hear the surf is in the east,
> and the surf is in the west, making a great stir with the two noises, and
> they hitting one on the other. I'll have no call now to be going down
> and getting Holy Water in the dark nights after Samhain, and I won't
> care what way the sea is when the other women will be keening. . . . It
> isn't that I haven't prayed for you, Bartley, to the Almighty God. It isn't
> that I haven't said prayers in the dark night till you wouldn't know
> what I'd be saying; but it's a great rest I'll have now, and it's time
> surely. It's a great rest I'll have now, and great sleeping in the nights
> after Samhain, if it's only a bit of wet flour we do have to eat, and
> maybe a fish that would be stinking (53).

Maurya is finding a little peace and consolation; but for an audience
this intensifies the tragedy—that in this life the only way to get rest
and comfort is through the death of loved ones, through the exhaus-
tion of all capacity for suffering. Yet at the end one feels that remarkable exultation which is at the heart of real tragedy. Having supped
pain and horror to the full and known the pitch of agony, Maurya
gets beyond the world, since she no longer has any claims upon it, nor
it upon her. Accordingly calm and compassion come to her, she

forgets herself and acquires humility and charity, and in her last words uttered as she stands up alone there is a predominant note of reconciliation and a new concern for others:

> They're all together this time, and the end is come. May the Almighty God have mercy on Bartley's soul, and on Michael's soul, and on the souls of Sheamus and Patch, and Stephen and Shawn (*bending her head*); and may He have mercy on my soul, Nora, and on the soul of every one is left living in the world. . . . Michael has a clean burial in the far north, by the grace of the /190/ Almighty God. Bartley will have a fine coffin out of the white boards, and a deep grave surely. What more can we want than that? No man at all can be living for ever, and we must be satisfied.

Integral to this is the theme of dream versus actuality. The dream is the hope that one may escape the sea; the actuality is the sea or death; though nightmare would probably be a more accurate word than dream to apply to the side of the tension opposite to the sea or death. For the hopes, the dream, of such a person as Maurya are from time to time shattered by the actuality, the sea or death. Her life is a continual alternation between hope that someone will escape the sea or death and the fear that no one will escape. Unlike the figures of *The Well of the Saints,* who are normally able to ignore harsh actuality and enjoy a tolerable life in the dream, the islanders cannot rest in the dream. The islanders' dream is constantly turning to nightmare as actuality remorselessly intrudes with the death of a dear one at sea. Nevertheless, while some men are still alive, the islanders must go on hoping, must believe in the dream. And if no deaths occur for a while, and the men are able to make a little money by their labour, the islanders can enjoy their festivals and customs and delight in some of the good things of life. But there is a further twist of pain in the fact that they can only have these material necessities of life, and a little more if lucky, through the sacrifice of men. Men must risk their lives to keep all alive; the cost in human life and suffering merely to maintain the existence of the community is enormous, but unless one wants to lie down and die without an effort, this cost must be paid. Hence arises the terrible dilemma that if a woman has, like Maurya, several men in the family, she has a good chance of always having enough to eat at least, but she has also constant anxiety about their safety, and recurrent agony as one by one the sea devours them. Without sons or men one is spared the worry but one goes short of the necessities of life; one has only 'a bit of wet flour' and 'maybe a fish that would be stinking'. Thus in *Riders to the Sea* horror comes from the fact that no one can rest in the

dream; it is shattered from time to time by actuality—the sea or
death. All know that the dream may only be a dream, that no one
may escape actuality, yet they must go on believing in the dream,
there is nothing else short of emigration or suicide; and /191/ this
constant tension between the dream (that one may escape) and the
many evidences around proving that hardly anyone will escape,
makes worry and restlessness endemic to life. As Synge says:[3]

> The maternal feeling is so powerful on these islands that it gives a life
> of torment to the women. Their sons grow up to be banished as soon
> as they are of age, or to live here in continual danger on the sea; their
> daughters go away also, or are worn out in their youth with bearing
> children that grow up to harass them in their own turn a little later.

The tension is always present in some degree until the time when
the dream is finally extinguished. This occurs when no one has
escaped, and there is no need to dream further: 'there isn't anything
more the sea can do'. At this stage the tension disappears, and one
sees actuality as it is—the sea or death. From the ending of this
tension and from the contemplation of the actuality behind all ap-
pearances and dreams, comes a new state of calm acquiescence,
humility and compassion; the mood of Maurya's last speech: 'No man
at all can be living for ever, and we must be satisfied.' The horror
goes out of life—one has been through the worst—but with it go both
the motive and the means of life, and only rest and oblivion remain.

Yeats says:[4] 'The old woman in *The Riders to the Sea* in mourning
for her six fine sons, mourns for the passing of all beauty and strength.'
I think this is true. Our consideration of this play, of all Synge's
writings, and of his life, gives us cause to entertain the suggestion that
although Maurya is primarily both an individual—a mother living in
a particular place at a particular time—and also representative of the
enduring characteristics of her kind, she is also something else. She
represents not only all the Aran islanders but also all humanity.
She is an image of humanity facing a hostile universe, and through
her Synge hints, as he does in other ways, that life is essentially tragic
and the final reality is death, and that through the acceptance of this
fact, along with compassion for doomed humanity, charity and peace
may come.

---

[3] *The Aran Islands* (Dublin, 1912), pp. 111-112.
[4] *Essays* (London, 1924), p. 383.

Thomas F. Van Laan

Form as Agent in Synge's
*Riders to the Sea**

John Millington Synge's *Riders to the Sea* combines simplicity of
action with complexity of form to achieve its unique and intense
effect. The action of its few minutes' playing time confines itself to
the helpless submission of Maurya, in what is emphatically established as the last of a series of capitulations, to the antagonist which
relentlessly opposes her. This simplicity in the action accounts in part
for the play's rare intensity; but a full accounting requires examination of two further, closely related aspects of the play: the identity
of Maurya's antagonist and Synge's method of establishing it. Her
antagonist is most frequently identified as the sea, because it is in the
sea that her husband and children have been drowned, and it is
the sea which during the present action takes Bartley, the only remaining son. Yet despite the sea's archetypal significance for mankind, this
identification seems scarcely adequate to explain the overwhelming
emotion universally resulting from a performance of *Riders to the
Sea*, especially since the sea here exists only as a verbal reference
somehow affecting a visible and thus more immediate action.[1] Apparently sensing this inadequacy, U. M. Ellis-Fermor, although pointing
out that "it is the sea that is the real theme of the play," prefers to
call the force opposing Maurya "Nature."[2] The advantage of her

* Reprinted from *Drama Survey*, III (Winter, 1964), 352-365, by permission of
the author. Copyright 1964 by *Drama Survey*.
[1] The possible inadequacy of the merely verbal reference will be appreciated
by those who have seen Robert Flaherty's documentary "Man of Aran" (1934).
Here the sea, one of the most powerful visual images ever recorded, completely
dominates both man and island.

[2] *The Irish Dramatic Movement*, Second Edition (London, 1954), p. 169.

term lies in its evocation of a realm at once including the sea and yet
vaster, at once manifesting itself in concretions like the sea yet also
suggesting something intangible which transcends them. The disad-
vantage of the term is that of all such abstractions: it lacks precise
definition. The question of the nature of Maurya's antagonist and its
contribution to the play's intensity cannot be resolved without consideration of the other major aspect of the play, its complex form.
Criticism of *Riders to the Sea* has continually turned to the subject of
form; the play's uniqueness has been correlated with its lyrical inspiration, its "preternatural intensity," its "deep sense of inevitableness," its "swiftness," and its "hard condensation."[3] The complexity
with which Synge has worked out the embodiment of his simple
action deserves far more analysis than it has yet received. For it is
/353/ the individual elements of the play's form—its brevity, its
bleakness of development, its inevitability, its constant pre-enactment
of the culminating moment of the whole play, and its suppression of
individuality—which actually define the various qualities comprising
Maurya's antagonist. Moreover, in the integration of these numerous
elements the form acquires the complexity, rigidity, and supremacy
that make it a fitting container for the fusion of these defined qualities and hence a prominent, active agent in the dramatic conflict.

Probably the most immediately apparent feature of the play's
form is brevity. Shorter than the usual one-act play, *Riders to the Sea*
automatically impresses reader and spectator alike with its brevity,
and Synge intensifies the effect by restricting his natural lyric bent.
The speeches, as P. P. Howe has noted, lack the rhythmical expan-
sion characteristic of Synge's prose in the other plays.[4] Although this
truncating is most apparent in the first half, Synge prolongs it suffi-
ciently to emphasize the rapid movement from voice to voice, with
the result that the action seems to race to its culmination. The unusual brevity of *Riders to the Sea* has prompted one of the few
attacks upon its structure. Howe regrets that Synge has created such
an obvious disparity between the actual playing time and the time
demanded by the off-stage events, especially the drowning of Bartley.[5]
But the discrepancy is so apparent that if naturalism were Synge's

---

[3] Ronald Peacock, *The Poet in the Theatre* (New York, 1960), p. 110; L. A. G.
Strong, *John Millington Synge* (London, 1941), p. 29; Maurice Bourgeois, *John
Millington Synge and the Irish Theatre* (London, 1913), p. 161; P. P. Howe, *J. M.
Synge. A Critical Study* (New York, 1912), p. 58; Ellis-Fermor, p. 175. See also
Alan Price, *Synge and Anglo-Irish Drama* (London, 1961), pp. 181-191.

[4] Howe, p. 57.

[5] Howe, pp. 59-60.

primary concern he would not have permitted it. L. A. G. Strong
more perceptively compares this disparity in time with that in the
final scene of *Dr. Faustus* and concludes that "from its first words
this is a play acted against time. . . ."[6] As in Marlowe's play, the disparity between the two time schemes is clearly designed to emphasize
the *non*-natural swiftness with which events occur. Synge uses a
further device to heighten a spectator's awareness of the unusual
brevity. Near the beginning Nora quotes the young priest's assurance
that Michael, if dead, has received "a clean burial by the grace of
God"[7] (p. 83). The double repetition of this phrase, by Cathleen at
the climax (p. 93) and by Maurya at the end (p. 97), links more
decisively the opening and closing, stressing their virtual simultaneity.
The sense of brevity, thus emphasized, acts to contain its antithesis,
the sense that much has occurred. The combination yields to the
play's total form the impression of a force of sufficient potency to
accomplish so swiftly such thorough devastation.

As if to preserve the swiftness of his action, Synge has restricted
its development. The steady movement toward the ultimate conclusion rarely pauses to focus upon specific details, but the few /354/
details which Synge has introduced are heavily charged with significance. The general result is twofold: the bleakness of development
keeps the meaning of the play oriented in the sequence of events;
yet each detail potentially acts as a symbol of that meaning, as, for
example, the constant visual image of the new boards leaning against
the wall comes to represent not only the coffin of Michael but also
that of Bartley and of all those who died long before the present
action. A more particular result also derives from the paucity of
details, because in limiting them Synge has been able to establish a
precise relationship between two contrasting groups of detail that is
itself a definition of the conflict enacted in the sequence of events.
The nets, oil-skins, and new boards of the opening picture are aug-
mented, as the action develops, by the introduction of further concrete
objects: the bundle, the turf, the rope, the shirt, and the stitches.
Cathleen's initial activity (kneading and spinning) introduces a pattern of archetypal human actions which Synge later expands with
Maurya's stirring the fire and with the various comings and goings
to which the characters give so much attention. The concrete objects
and the archetypal actions combine to evoke the austerity and sim-

---

[6] Strong, pp. 29-30.

[7] All quotations from Synge's works are from *The Complete Works of John M.
Synge* (New York, 1935).

plicity of human life as it is here pictured. In contrast, the play's
remaining details develop the sense of Nature originally suggested
by the association which nets and oil-skins have with the sea. Synge
establishes the relevance of this second dimension through the verbal
motif of the almost monotonous references to wind, sea, and tide. By
restricting his details of human life to objects and actions that are a
visible part of the production, Synge has effectively emphasized the
invisible quality of his second dimension. Because these elements of
Nature remain invisible, they remain mysterious and awesome, not
comprehensible from the point of view of the visible and uncompli-
cated human dimension. The distinction is stressed when the human
speaker sees in the realm of Nature images expressing his own fears:
the "star up against the moon" (p. 86), "the black hags that do be
flying on the sea" (p. 91). When Synge brings the two dimensions
together in a single image, he shows the precise relationship between
the two. The nets and oil-skins represent man's attempts to work
upon Nature, but the other combined images show the futility of
such attempts. The invisible wind blows open the door (p. 84). The
pig with the black feet, mentioned only, has been eating the new bit
of rope, an object visible in the action (p. 85). In the principal image
combining the two realms (the twice-mentioned floating man, pp. 90,
91), the human has been destroyed by Nature, the visible has /355/
been made invisible. Thus, while the bleakness of development forces
attention on the sequence of events, the careful ordering of the few
details that are admitted conveys the invisible, mysterious nature of
the potent force governing that sequence.

Synge's presentation of the sequence of events adds further elements to the play's total form and thus provides further characteristics of Maurya's antagonist. One of the most emphatic qualities of
the action is the unquestionable inevitability of its outcome. From the
first moment the spectator realizes that tragedy will take place; he
very quickly knows as well the concrete shape the tragedy will assume. The first speech—Nora's "Where is she?"—immediately arouses
concern, for it initiates the continuous pattern through which Synge
seeks sympathy for his suffering victim. The speech even assumes
tragic import as Synge develops its context. Cathleen's reactions with
the spinning wheel make Nora's bundle portentous. The fearful protest that the shirt and stocking could not be Michael's tends rather
to assure the audience that they definitely are. With this sense of
impending disaster established in the opening moments, Synge then
proceeds to anticipate the death of Bartley so thoroughly that it becomes a foregone conclusion. Merciless repetition converts the priest's

assurance that "the Almighty God won't leave her destitute . . . with no son living" (p. 84) into cynical irony: the emphasis on the single remaining son in Maurya's "one son only" and Bartley's "but one man to work" (p. 86) pre-substantiates Maurya's fear that "when the black night is falling I'll have no son left me in the world" (p. 87). Maurya's prediction of Bartley's death has the force of fore-knowledge because she speaks to him of "the day you're drownd'd with the rest" as if it has already occurred, and with resigned cer-tainty she tells Nora and Cathleen: "He's gone now, God spare us, and we'll not see him again." Bartley's own indefiniteness about the time of his return suggests that he too is partially aware, and implies that a force with greater knowledge than that of the characters uses them as mouthpiece. This possibility ramifies when Nora and Cath-leen both remark that Bartley will be "destroyed" (p. 88). They mean, of course, that he has left without eating, but Synge's addi-tional, superior meaning is abundantly clear in the context and is made even more clear when Cathleen repeats the word in its fuller sense after Maurya has described her vision of Michael (p. 93). With Bartley gone, Nora and Cathleen discover that the clothes in the bundle are indeed Michael's, and this fulfillment of an anticipated outcome ensures that Bartley's death, so thoroughly anticipated, must /356/ also be fulfilled. All good drama creates similar forward move-ments, similar patterns of anticipation and fulfillment, but seldom is the outcome as inexorably predetermined as in *Riders to the Sea*. This pronounced inevitability adds to the play a sense of necessity and compulsion which is reinforced by other devices. The priest's un-hesitating decision not to stop Bartley suggests that the attempt would be futile. When Bartley enters, he is "in a hurry" (p. 85), as if driven; his double insistence that he "must go now quickly" (pp. 86, 87) suggests that he acts under an agency other than his own will. Through this sense of the inevitability and the necessity of the out-come, Synge establishes the overwhelming helplessness of his char-acters before the powerful, invisible antagonist whose will, even though known, cannot be thwarted by human efforts.

Synge emphasizes the helplessness anew in a further formal em-bodiment of his sequence of events. The demands of plot require that individual moments which prepare for the climaxes be given some kind of visible enactment. These are the real "obligatory scenes" when the basic point of the drama lies in the outcome, in the climax itself, as it does in *Riders to the Sea*. The great dramatist makes such requisite preparatory scenes do double duty: not only is the necessary information given but also, through the manner in which it is con-

veyed, the essence of the later important climactic moment is already
established. Both the significance and the validity of the outcome are
thus inherent throughout the drama. In *Riders to the Sea*, Synge
masterfully utilizes this dramatic technique of making almost every
scene epitomize the whole action. The general sequence of events
traces the cornering and defeat of Maurya by her antagonist; the
separate moments which lead up to this outcome are again and again
enactments of Maurya's helplessness before opposition. The first indication of Maurya's situation—Cathleen's "She's lying down, God
help her, and may be sleeping, if she's able" (p. 83)—at once casts
doubt upon her capacity to cope with circumstances. Maurya herself
heightens this impression by continually mentioning her age. Synge
has her "raking the fire aimlessly" (p. 88), which suggests her helplessness in performing one of life's basic actions. Again, she is "hard
set . . . to walk," yet without protest yields to the girls' urging that
she carry Bartley's food down to the spring well. The accumulating
impressions make her action of putting "up her hands, as if to hide
something from her eyes" (p. 93) seem to be a characteristic gesture.
The helplessness evoked by these incidental effects, the quality which
epitomizes her whole role in the one-sided battle with her antagonist,
/357/ gets fuller elaboration in the two battles which Synge makes a
visible part of his action. The first battle, in which Nora and Cathleen
oppose Maurya, is as pathetically one-sided as the major defeat because Maurya does not even know she is in conflict. The contest pits
the girls' desire to keep hidden from her the truth about Michael
against their fear that she will discover it. Synge twice brings Maurya
on the scene when the bundle is in evidence, but each time the girls
easily hide it before she can see it, and Maurya does not learn of the
concrete proof of Michael's death until she already knows of it
through her vision and through seeing the body of Bartley. Synge's
point is doubly made: Maurya's futility is indicated by the ease with
which knowledge of importance can be kept from her; the insignifi-
cant delay brought about by the girls' efforts generalizes the principle
to show the futility of struggle in itself. The second battle, that between Maurya and Bartley, has far more importance, because Maurya
knows she is struggling and therefore dedicates all her efforts. Thus
her defeat is more revealing. This battle has its own preliminary as
Maurya tries to prevent Bartley from taking the bit of new rope
(p. 85). He ignores her plea, not even bothering to reply until she has
tried further persuasion. But in the battle proper, when Maurya
vainly urges him to stay, she has not even this token victory: no mat-

ter what Maurya says, Bartley speaks only to Cathleen or Nora. Her defeat in this epitome of the main battle with the antagonist is total. Thus, through this aspect of his form, pre-enactment, Synge succeeds in showing how pertinent to the play's meaning is her ultimate defeat. The epitome also brings into sharper focus her weakness in the face of opposition, and since Bartley represents an opponent who is familiar and visible rather than awesome and mysterious, what is weakness and ineffectualness in the epitome must be abject helplessness in the action as a whole. Finally, Bartley's aloofness, his complete disregard for Maurya's feelings, and his apparent indifference to her existence help Synge present in the concrete terms of the theatre some of the characteristic attributes of her invisible antagonist.

As the girls' futile efforts to hide Michael's death from Maurya attest, Synge traces her helplessness not as an individual trait but as a representation of the general human condition. A further element of the play's form increases this sense of the insignificance of the individual when facing the antagonist. Synge so arranges his action that Michael and Bartley become united, that the death of one is the death of the other. The play begins as a search for the missing, probably dead, Michael; it ends with the discovery and return of the body, /358/ but the body is Bartley's. Within this larger pattern Synge also effects other, more explicit links between the two brothers. The girls' attempt to find Michael—their examination of the bundle—gives prominent focus to the flannel shirt of the drowned man. During his brief appearance, Bartley "takes off his old coat, and puts on a newer one of the same flannel" (p. 87). When the girls try to compare the shirt from the bundle with one of Michael's, they find not Michael but Bartley, for it is Michael's shirt that he has worn (p. 90). Thus even before Bartley's death, the ironic result of the search and the shirt itself establish the close relationship between the two brothers as victims. Synge makes the association far more explicit when Bartley has been drowned. As the women perform their ritual entrance, an announcement of death, Maurya asks, "Is it Patch, or Michael, or what is it at all?" (p. 94). Cathleen then tells her, for the first time, that Michael has been drowned "in the far north, and when he is found there how could he be here in this place?" For Maurya, Bartley and Michael are linked in death, because she learns of both drownings simultaneously. But the most significant linking for the audience comes through Synge's language. When Maurya disputes Cathleen's assurance—for it could be anybody there in the north—Cathleen insists, "It's Michael. . . ." At this point the "it" receives a concrete reference as the men carry in the body of Bartley, and at the same time the "it" denoting Michael dissolves into an "it" denoting Bartley: to Cathleen's question, "Is it Bartley it is?" one of the women replies, "It is surely, God rest his soul." The dissolving of one into the other is then complete when Maurya "drops Michael's clothes across Bartley's feet. . . ." (p. 96). The drowned man's clothes return to their owner.

Synge's most deliberate attempt to link Michael and Bartley comes in the moment of death itself through the symbol of the horses. Bartley is going to Galway to sell horses and thus the symbol is introduced early in the play (p. 84). The repetitions are numerous: Bartley will ride down to the shore on the mare; Maurya compares the price of a thousand horses to the one remaining son; Bartley establishes the pattern of the two specific horses of the symbol, the red mare which he will ride, the gray pony which is to run behind him (pp. 86, 87). Synge clearly creates this elaborate preparation in order to ensure a full audience participation in the significance of Maurya's vision. Cathleen's renewal of the red mare-gray pony pattern re-establishes the importance of the whole motif just at the moment when Maurya is to tell how in pursuing Bartley she "looked up then . . . at the gray pony, and there was Michael upon it" (p. 93). /359/ Her immediate conclusion, "Bartley will be lost now," expresses one significance of the horse symbol, the linking of her two sons in death. The whole pattern which doubles Michael and Bartley as one individual magnifies the power of the antagonist in a rather morbid mathematical ratio. The pattern simultaneously adds to the de-emphasis of the individual: in the face of such power the human is helpless. Yet the horse symbol has an even more complex function in defining the antagonist than the mere linking of the two sons. Bartley's death is weird, mysterious, not only because of the eerie references to horses, but also and more importantly because while Michael and the others have gone to the sea to be drowned, in the death of Bartley the sea reaches out for its victim. Maurya's vision even suggests that Michael in some way has helped the sea accomplish its act of destruction: the antagonist enlists its victims as agents in the crushing of new victims. The weirdness of Bartley's death demonstrates quite emphatically that the antagonist is not merely impassive and aloof, destroying that which disturbs its domain. In taking Bartley, it shows itself to be an active pursuer. This malevolent implication occurs once more when in Maurya's memory of the drowning of Patch, she recalls the dripping sea water making a track from the door on into the house, as if the

sea were in further pursuit of its most recent victim.[8] The horse
symbol contributes yet one more effect to Synge's delineation of the
antagonist. Jan Setterquist has suggested an association between
Synge's horses and the White Horses of Ibsen's *Rosmersholm*.[9] Influence remains to be shown with any conclusiveness, yet the comparison
is suggestive. Synge's horses, especially in company with the vision of
Michael, add to the antagonist of *Riders to the Sea* the same sense
of supernatural indestructibility that the White Horses of *Rosmersholm* give to the past and its traditions. But in *Rosmersholm* it is not
merely the mention of the symbol that gives it its power; rather it is
Rebecca's gradual but sure recognition of the White Horses' reality.
In like fashion, Synge's horses enhance the invisible mysteriousness
and unrestrained power of the antagonist most conclusively and
effectively when one of the women tells Cathleen how Bartley was
drowned: "The gray pony knocked him into the sea, and he was
washed out where there is a great surf on the white rocks" (p. 95).

In the climactic speeches of the play—Maurya's recounting of the
destruction the antagonist has brought to her family (pp. 93-94)—the
implications established by the various elements of form are /360/
given a verbal equivalent. These two speeches are especially valuable
for their achieving a characterization of human life when it is at the
mercy of a force so powerful, inevitable, mysterious, and consistent.
In reviving the motifs of "the sea" and "the great wind" and in
focusing upon the "dark night," her speeches establish the influence
in the destruction of her family of the force and its mystery. With
such an antagonist the story of her family's existence naturally
assumes the pattern of death followed by death followed by death
until, as Denis Donoghue notes, "the creativity of the family is
broken, only the women are left."[10] That some of the men were never
even found emphasizes the futility of their existence. But the major
statement of the intrinsic futility comes through the subtle pattern
in her speeches of repeated references to wood and wooden objects.
This pattern forms a verbal image which fixes the meaning of the
constant presence of the new boards leaning against the wall. Since
Bartley will now be lost, Maurya requests, "let you call in Eamon and

---

[8] Cf. Denis Donoghue, "Synge: 'Riders to the Sea': A Study," *University Review*,
I (1955), 56: "The track of water in these situations becomes a symbol of the way
by which Death comes, from the sea straight to the house, to the family."
[9] *Ibsen and the Beginnings of Anglo-Irish Drama: I. John Millington Synge*
(Upsala, 1951), p. 32.
[10] Donoghue, p. 55.

make me a good coffin out of the white boards. . . ." She recalls how
Stephen and Shawn were "carried up the two of them on the one
plank," how "not a stick or sign" was seen of the lost Sheamus and
his father, how Patch "after was drowned out of a curagh that turned
over," with the board image here suggested in the wooden ribs that
form the boat's framework. The climax of this image pattern occurs,
of course, when immediately afterward, "men carry in the body of
Bartley, laid on a plank. . . ." (p. 95). The fusion of the verbal and
the visual completes Synge's uniting of each of the victims through
the board image. The effect is rendered more complex by the actual
presence of the boards: when first seen they suggest the possibility of
creation—a new table perhaps; but the spectator soon realizes that
the only thing ever to be built from these boards is a coffin, a coffin
originally intended for Michael, here chosen by Maurya, and ultimately consigned to Bartley. Fresh, new boards are a potential symbol
of a minor success in man's perpetual struggle to convert the objects
of Nature to his own use. But in *Riders to the Sea* the boards suggest
rather that man's struggles yield him only the housing for his corpse.

Maurya's speeches carry the play's statement about the futility of
human life to its ultimate through Synge's careful juxtaposition of its
two extremes, birth and death. Although Maurya's purpose is to summarize the deaths of her "six fine men," she prefaces the summary
with "though it was a hard birth I had with every one of them
and they coming to the world." The second speech reaches its climax
in /361/ her memory of Bartley as "a baby, lying on my two knees" at
the time when the women had entered to announce the death of Patch.
And in the action of the play, the vision of Bartley the baby is immediately followed by the bringing in of Bartley the corpse. Synge
has previously suggested the validity of this juxtaposition with his
image of "the dead man with the child in his arms" (p. 92) : life
under these circumstances seems only a birth immediately followed
by a death; birth itself presupposes death. Once again Maurya is pro-
viding a verbal equivalent of an aspect of form, because Synge has
apparently peopled his play with only the very young and the very
old. The young priest mentioned at the beginning receives his antithesis in the Old Man at the end. The first group of women mourners
is old, the second young. The conflicts presented in the action are
conflicts between the young and the old, as Synge indicates through
Cathleen's observation on the struggle between Bartley and Maurya:
"It's the life of a young man to be going on the sea, and who would
listen to an old woman with one thing and she saying it over?"
(p. 87). Synge establishes a similar effect in a formal juxtaposition

of the youthful dead and the elderly living: taking Michael's stick, Maurya remarks that "in this place it is the young men do be leaving things behind for them that do be old" (p. 89) ; as she prepares to relate her vision of Bartley and Michael, she "starts, so that her shawl falls back from her head and shows her white tossed hair" (p. 92) ; the Old Man is chosen to build the coffin for Bartley.

Finally, Maurya's speeches assist other statements in enhancing that aspect of form which expresses the power of the antagonist by multiplying its victims. The linking of Michael and Bartley is echoed in Maurya's pairing of Stephen and Shawn. When she recounts the loss of "Sheamus and his father, and his own father again," the doubling has become a tripling. The board motif dissolves them all into one blurred group, a process heightened by Maurya's reaction to the women's ritual entrance—"Is it Patch, or Michael, or what is it at all?" (p. 94)—and by an onlooker's remark about "all the coffins she's seen made already" (p. 97). But the multiplication of victims assumes even greater importance, for it eventually includes all men everywhere. From the first, others, outside the family group, are involved in Bartley's fate (pp. 85, 86). The sign recording Michael's death (his shirt) has for its signification "many another man" as well (p. 90). The relevance of "the others" acquires its dramatic embodiment when the women and men begin to file in in groups. The ritual nature of the women's mourning indicates that it /362/ is recurrent, not isolated, a general lament for all their dead, not a particular grief for Maurya's loss. Synge completes his universalizing of the victim from the individual to the family to man in general when Maurya expands the account of her own loss so that it may accommodate all loss, yet still explain it in terms of sea and wind: "There does be a power of young men floating round in the sea, and what way would they know if it was Michael they had, or another man like him, for when a man is nine days in the sea, and the wind blowing, it's hard set his own mother would be to say what man was it" (p. 95). The universalizing implies that the point of the play cannot be limited to a single family on a small island in the west of Ireland. More important, as the individual yields his significance to become a part of one mass victim, the absolute omnipotence of the antagonist emerges beyond question. And this final rejection of the validity of the individual accounts for the one aspect of form not yet considered, an aspect often noted but most fully treated by R. L. Collins, the virtual non-existence of concrete individuality in the characters.[11] Here the

---

[11] "The Distinction of *Riders to the Sea*," *The University of Kansas City Review*, XIII (1947), 278-284.

major character may serve as the primary example. Maurya projects only age and defeat, memory and capitulation. Synge's purpose is evident toward the end of the play when Cathleen defines the nature of her mother's capitulation, for she alters the specific reference, "It's getting old she is, and broken," to the general application, "An old woman will be soon tired with anything she will do. . . ." (p. 97). Maurya is not just the mother of Michael and Bartley, of Shawn and Patch; in Donoghue's words, "she is the Mother, the pathetic custodian of the family-unit."[12] These characters are not meant to be specific because they have the more important function of being typical. That Maurya's defeat by her antagonist is the defeat of us all Synge shows through the inclusiveness of the play's final line: *"No man at all* can be living for ever, and *we* must be satisfied" (p. 97).[13]

The Irish dramatic movement produced a theory of tragedy which establishes in critical precept what Synge effected dramatically. In his essay on "The Tragic Theatre" (1910), Yeats denies that "dogma of the printed criticism" which asserts "that the dramatic moment is always the contest of character with character." For Yeats, character— by which he means "personality," the individualized creature of the "real world"—belongs only to comedy or tragicomedy. In tragedy, on the other hand, "all is lyricism, unmixed passion, 'the integrity of fire.' " Thus, "tragedy must always be a drowning and breaking of the dykes that separate man from man"; in tragedy "the /363/ persons upon the stage, let us say, greaten till they are humanity itself."[14] Yeats's theory cannot be definitely linked to Synge's practice, but it is nevertheless a remarkably succinct expression of the principle by which Synge suppresses individuality in order to make his Maurya representative of the plight of all mankind. Even more remarkable is the movement's agreement upon a further reason for the elimination of "character" in Yeats's sense. While developing his theory in 1909, Yeats wrote that "A poet creates tragedy from his own soul, that soul which is alike in all men. It has not joy, as we understand that word, but ecstasy, which is from the contemplation of things vaster than the individual and imperfectly seen, perhaps, by all those that still live."[15] Lady Gregory expresses a similar principle in more

---

12 Donoghue, p. 56.

13 Italics added.

14 W. B. Yeats, *Essays* (New York, 1924), pp. 296-303. The equation of character with personality appears in "The Death of Synge," *Dramatis Personae* (New York, 1936), pp. 127-128. See "Estrangement: Extracts from a Diary Kept in 1909" (*Dramatis Personae,* pp. 95-96) for an earlier development of the ideas expressed in 1910.

15 "Estrangement," p. 96.

prosaic words in the notes to her *New Irish Comedies* (1913): "Fate itself is the protagonist, your actor cannot carry much character, it is out of place. You do not want to know the character of a wrestler you see trying his strength at a show."[16] It is this focus upon a protagonist mightier than the human, this attempt to glimpse things vaster than the individual that constitutes the primary reason for the suppression of personality in *Riders to the Sea*. By sacrificing the development of character Synge makes the antagonist the central figure of his play.

And it is through the various elements of his form that Synge defines the nature of the antagonist. The bleakness of development and the suppression of human individuality suggest its unrestricted supremacy. The swiftness, the inevitability of outcome, the consistency of the action, and the epitomizing of life as birth and death indicate not only its unlimited power but also its unrelenting and malevolent pursuit of the human victims. The implications established by these various formal characteristics posit a supreme force which is awesome in its power and its malevolence, a force which is pagan rather than Christian, perhaps—and this the play emphatically suggests—even anti-Christian. Daniel Corkery misrepresents the play when he writes that here Synge "had to shed his little personal prejudices against the religion of the people," that he "shows himself as aware that sheer distraction must follow on such sense as was theirs of this malignancy if they had not as well a world over and beyond the warfare of wind and wave to rest their thoughts on."[17] For Synge shows that it is the consolation offered by Christianity which topples at the onslaught of this anti-Christian enemy. The Christian references in *Riders to the Sea* are numerous, and all suggest inadequacy and defeat. The priest is young. It is his assur- /364/ ance that "the Almighty God won't leave her destitute" which Synge makes ironic. He fails to stop Bartley. When Bartley has gone, Cathleen cries out in despair: "The Son of God forgive us, Nora, we're after forgetting his bit of bread" (p. 88). The ambiguous "his" subtly connotes the Eucharist, which Nora's immediate "And it's destroyed he'll be going till dark night" makes seem only an ineffectual piece of magic designed to ward off inevitable evil. When Maurya is told of the young priest's assurance, her age and experience reply, "It's little the like of him knows of the sea...." (p. 93). As she sprinkles Holy Water over Bartley, her speech indi-

---

16 Quoted by Ellis-Fermor, p. 66.

17 *Synge and Anglo-Irish Literature: A Study* (Cork University Press, 1931), pp. 108, 136. Cf. Donoghue's interpretation of this play as a drama of Christian Acceptance, pp. 52, 57.

cates the futility of prayer: "It isn't that I haven't prayed for you,
Bartley, to the Almighty God. It isn't that I haven't said prayers in
the dark night till you wouldn't know what I'ld be saying. . . ." (p. 96).
The Holy Water is used up, and Maurya's action of putting "the
empty cup mouth downwards on the table" (p. 97) visually represents
the defeat of Christianity as part of the total defeat. In the final
speech, Michael "has a clean burial in the far north, by the grace of
the Almighty God," but for Bartley there is only death, only "a fine
coffin out of the white boards, and a deep grave surely." As L. A. G.
Strong has remarked in reference to Maurya's rejection of the young
priest's assurance, "for these people there is but one almighty power.
. . ."[18] The treatment of Christianity presented in *Riders to the Sea*
is wholly in keeping with Synge's attitude in other works, with the
rejection of the Saint's interference in *The Well of the Saints*, with
the exposure of the priest's intrinsic lack of humanity in *The Tinker's
Wedding*, and with the tragic realization in *Deirdre of the Sorrows*
that youth and love are brief, that death offers no second, better life
to make up for the shortness of this life's joy. Probably the best
commentary on *Riders to the Sea's* dramatization of a hostile, anti-
Christian universe occurs in Synge's prose work, *The Aran Islands*.
The passage which discusses the keen ignores any suggestion of consolation; it focuses directly upon the supremacy of the antagonist
defined through form in the play: "In this cry of pain the inner
consciousness of the people seems to lay itself bare for an instant, and
to reveal the mood of beings who feel this isolation in the face of a
universe that wars on them with winds and seas. They are usually
silent, but in the presence of death all outward show of indifference
or patience is forgotten, and they shriek with pitiable despair before
the horror of the fate to which they all are doomed" (p. 346).[19]

For the islanders, and for Synge who shared their experience, mention of the sea would adequately call up this feeling of a warring /365/
universe. But to convey the feeling to his spectators Synge had to
create a medium more in keeping with the possibilities of the theatre.
Synge makes the experience of his islanders truly universal by creating a form so fully executed that it achieves the substantial reality of

---

[18] Strong, p. 32.

[19] In the sequel to this passage Synge makes explicit the irony with which he
views the islanders' Christianity in the play: "Before they covered the coffin an
old man kneeled down by the grave and repeated a simple prayer for the dead.
There was an irony in these words of atonement and Catholic belief spoken by
voices that were still hoarse with the cries of pagan desperation."

independent existence. For the primary characteristic of the play's form is not one or another of its various elements but rather the rich complexity resulting from the fusion of *all* elements. The various formal characteristics not only define; in uniting they establish a living essence which dominates the characters to become the leading actor of the play. By thus shaping his form, Synge has introduced an agent capable of embodying all the qualities of the antagonist and of sufficient substantiality to make the antagonist a felt part of the dramatic experience. The special achievement of *Riders to the Sea* lies in the manner in which Synge has successfully rendered the necessarily abstract and intangible in a presence seemingly as immediate and concrete as the more obviously tangible and visible elements of the theatre. Just as an actor provides the living reality that converts the verbal and visual signs of character into a single coherent image, the play's complex form provides an emotional structure suitably embodying the omnipotent force whose victim is human life.

Recognizing Synge's achievement, one must reject Miss Ellis-Fermor's conclusion about the "curious absence of metaphysical or religious implication" in Synge's tragedies.[20] There is, indeed, no speculative comment, no explicit probing; Synge has thoroughly dramatized every element of the experience: he has discovered the reality rather than asserted it. *Riders to the Sea* has been considered untragic because of the weakness of Maurya,[21] and because of the absence of any "implication of resolution."[22] But the play is tragic. Maurya is admittedly weak; although she can suffer, she can perceive little; yet, as Richard Sewall has pointed out, "in an age when the symbol of the hero as the dominating centre of the play seems to have lost its validity with artist and audience, the role is taken over by the artist himself, who is his own tragic hero. That is, 'perception' is conveyed more generally, in the total movement of the piece and through all its parts."[23] The observation is especially appropriate to *Riders to the Sea* because through form, through the total movement of the piece and all its parts, Synge has achieved perception, and in the fullness of that perception, no matter how frightening the prospect discovered, lies the resolution of tragedy.

---

[20] Ellis-Fermor, p. 185.
[21] Cf. Donoghue, p. 57: "Maurya's sufferings are determined by forces which do not include her will or her character."
[22] Ellis-Fermor, p. 185.
[23] "The Tragic Form," *Essays in Criticism*, IV (1954), p. 357.

Donna Gerstenberger

Riders to the Sea*

I The Whole Fabric

From *The Aran Islands*, which Synge called his "first serious piece of work," he learned "to write the peasant dialect and dialogue" which were to be so effective in his plays. The Aran Islands taught Synge a great deal more than his remarkable use of language, however, for out of his experiences of the Islands and the creation of a book about them came the sense of peasant life which pervades all the plays and gives to Synge coherent expression of his attitudes toward life. Nowhere is this sense of peasant life so evident in Synge's work as in *Riders to the Sea*, a play begun during the same summer as *In the Shadow of the Glen* but not staged until 1904, a year after Synge's first produced play had tried the boards of Molesworth Hall. The setting, the colors, the action, the attitudes, the symbols, the rhythms of the keening women, of fate, and of the sea—all these are present in *The Aran Islands*; and they are the raw materials which Synge compressed, fused, and shaped anew in the creation of the one-act tragedy *Riders to the Sea*.

The intense perfection of this short play stresses more than any other work the nature and quality of Synge's artistic accomplishment, although the bitter, society-directed irony of the comedies is not present; and, for this reason, *Riders to the Sea* holds in some respects a special place in relation to Synge's work as a whole. The sense of place and of a people is strong in this play, as in all Synge's plays; and, on one level, *Riders to the Sea* may be viewed (as the other plays

---

* Reprinted from *John Millington Synge*. New York: Twayne Publishers, Inc., 1964, pp. 44-54, by permission of the publisher. © 1964 by Twayne Publishers, Inc.

may not) as "folk drama," for there is none of the conflict here between the needs of the individual and the restrictive demands of
society, a conflict which becomes thematic material in most of the
other plays. /45/ Predictably enough, *Riders to the Sea* is the only
one of Synge's plays presented during his lifetime which did not
occasion angry denunciations from audiences in Ireland. In fact, according to Lennox Robinson in *Ireland's Abbey Theatre*, the recep-
tion of the play was largely an indifferent one.

Riders to the Sea does not concern itself with social issues; instead
it cuts behind the surface concerns of life to engage its characters in
the most elemental kind of struggle—that for existence. The theme
of the play is stated with an artistic finality which leaves no room for
argument, and the play succeeds because Synge has completely inte-
grated all its aspects. There are no holes in the fabric of the drama;
as in the best poetry there are no parts separable from the whole. It
is this play of all of Synge's for which Una Ellis-Fermor's judgment
of his particular genius seems most appropriate: "Synge is the only
great poetic dramatist of the [Irish] movement; the only one, that is,
for whom poetry and drama were inseparable, in whose work dramatic intensity invariably finds poetic expression and the poetic mood
its only full expression in dramatic form."[1]

The most immediate effect of *Riders to the Sea* is its sense of inevitability and economy. There is nothing that is extraneous; there is
nothing that is without meaning in a total pattern, a pattern which
works toward an almost symphonic integration of theme and expression. There is no insistence on Synge's part on his meaning; everything in the work grows out of the natural life which Synge observed
in the Aran Islands, and this realistic equivalent for all that happens
is a part of the play's inevitability and its art.

The scene is a simple one: "Cottage kitchen, with nets, oil-skins,
spinning-wheel, some new boards standing by the wall, etc." This is
the small world of the play, which will, before Synge has finished his
half hour on the stage, bring into the cottage the world beyond which
man cannot enclose, cannot control. All of the play is pervaded by a
sense of a large, natural atmosphere—of the elemental presence of
sky and landscape, shore and sea, storm and rocks—although the
whole scene is limited to the confines of the cottage kitchen. The immediate canvas is small, but the picture Synge presents has tragic
intensity and depth. The sea, which has claimed the lives of all of the
men of the family, fills the small kitchen with its presence, /46/ just

---

[1] *The Irish Dramatic Movement* (London, 1954), p. 163.

as it fills it with death before the quiet resignation with which the play ends—a quiet which the audience feels in the cessation of struggle like a silence on the sea itself at the storm's end.

In every aspect of his play, Synge has introduced the microcosm-macrocosm relationship. The cottage kitchen is a small world which contains the puny attempts of man to make a home of the large, alien world of the sea. And the island itself, surrounded by the unfriendly sea, becomes a paradigm for life, but one in which the bitter demands of existence speak with foreshortened insistence: "In the big world the old people do be leaving things after them for their sons and children, but in this place it is the young men do be leaving things behind for them that do be old." All men are riders to the sea, as the audience is reminded by an echo of the conclusion of Sophocles' *Oedipus* in Maurya's final words: "No man at all can be living for ever, and we must be satisfied."

The three women in the play, who are reminiscent of the three Fates of mythology, are an analogy ironic and meaningful in their *inability* to control; but Synge makes his comment effective precisely because he does not insist upon it. It is a parallel which, like many factors in the play, operates without an insistence upon a conscious awareness on the part of the audience. The three women can only endure, await the deprivation and loss which is their lot at the edge of the sea. Nevertheless, the play opens with Cathleen at the spinning wheel, spinning rapidly, as Nora brings in the shirt and stocking found on a drowned man. The clothing is identified as that belonging to their brother Michael, for Nora had dropped four stitches in the knitting of his stocking. The presence of the spinning woman and the attention given to the dropped stitches recalls the classical analogue in a persistent way throughout the play. The pattern of fate is being spun and woven as inexorably in *Riders to the Sea* as in any Classical tragedy, and Synge has provided the dramatic symbol, the stage equivalent, which is inevitable, natural, and right. In the same unobtrusive manner, we have the cutting of the knot on the bundle of clothing brought from the sea. "Give me a knife, Nora; the string's perished with the salt water, and there's a black knot on it you wouldn't loosen in a week." The shadows of Clotho, Lachesis, /47/ and Atropos quietly rise behind the figures of Synge's fate-ridden women.

Synge's symbolism is not only Classical in origin, it is also specifically Christian in its evocation. The source of the vision that Maurya sees of the drowned Michael riding behind the son soon to die may be found in *The Aran Islands* in a story about an accident in loading horses on a hooker; in it an old woman saw her drowned son riding on one of the horses, which was caught by a young man who was, then, himself drowned in the sea. Like almost everything in *Riders to the Sea*, the raw material for this incident is present in *The Aran Islands*, but in the prose work Synge presents an unimpassioned telling, which is unified, focused, and given wider context for the purposes of his dramatic recreation. In Maurya's vision of Bartley on the red mare, followed on the gray pony by Michael, already nine days drowned in the far north, Synge uses the Aran material to invoke wider echoes for his audience—those of the horsemen of the Book of Revelation: "And I looked, and behold a pale horse; and his name that sat on him was Death."

Bartley's death is for Maurya at this moment an accomplished fact, and she withholds from him the loaf which she has taken to the spring well to give him. Again, and very importantly, there is no insistence by Synge upon the pattern of meaning which is being worked out on a symbolic level, but it is operative, all the more effectively because of its inevitability on a naturalistic level. The bread is the bread of life—"And it's destroyed he'll be going till dark night, and he after eating nothing since the sun went up"—on any level one may choose. And it is, further, the pathetic attempt of the cottage kitchen to comfort and sustain the riders to the sea—the hopeless attempt of the small world to reach into the large.

The holy water which Maurya sprinkles over Bartley's dead body and over Michael's clothes out of the sea invokes Christian symbolism placed in as ironic a context by the play as the presentation of the three Fates. The drops of holy water are themselves pathetic reminders of the implacable appetite of the waters of the sea and of the meaningless reassurance of the young priest that "the Almighty God won't leave her destitute with no son living." There are no sons left, and Maurya's turning of the empty cup "mouth downwards on the table" enforces the /48/ resignation of her words: "They're all gone now, and there isn't anything more the sea can do to me."

Water has become, in the course of the play, perversely identified with death, not with life or regeneration. Maurya's failure to give Bartley blessing and bread occurs by the spring well, the source of lifegiving water, as opposed to the life-depriving waters of the sea, and the drops of holy water, within the context Synge has set for his play, become ironic reminders of man's frail hopes. The desolation is reminiscent of the early scene Synge draws in *The Aran Islands*, with the lonely stone crosses standing against the torrents of gray water, pitifully invoking "a prayer for the soul of the person they commemorated," but it is a desolation particularized, given embodiment upon the stage, even in the moment Maurya reaches out with her prayer to include humanity: "and may He have mercy on my soul, Nora, and on the soul of every one is left living in the world."

Synge weaves a pattern of poetic meaning into the colors he brings to his stage, both in the speech and in the setting of the play, as a part of the heightened effect of his play. Of these, red is the most effectively used, and the repetition of this color takes on the kind of implications which we have come to expect in poetry, where the inter-action of sensory impressions is closer and more intense than one ordinarily expects in prose. The red mare which Bartley rides to his death is linked in the imagination not only with Revelation but also with the red sail in which Patch was brought home while Bartley was a child upon Maurya's lap (Bartley's body is, of course, brought home in a piece of sail). The identification of the color is given its most dramatically convincing statement in the red petticoats which the old women pull over their heads as they keen and sway for Bartley's death. Red is the color of blood, the color of sacrifice; here, the color of grief. Synge had noted in *The Aran Islands* that the red dresses of the women provided a joy unknown to anyone "who has not lived for weeks among these grey clouds and seas." The gray sea has triumphed, however, in *Riders to the Sea;* and the dresses become one more reminder of the frailty of man in his joy and his sorrow.

Less insistent but equally operative are other color contexts. The white boards which stand on the stage from the opening /49/ of the curtain are fine ones bought for the making of Michael's coffin, which are pressed into service for Bartley's at the end of the play. And when the girls discuss the state of the sea by the white rocks, the audience is prepared for the identification of the color with death, for it is by the white rocks that Bartley will be drowned. Black is also consistently used in the play, perhaps more in its usual connotation than in the case of the other colors; for it is a "black" knot on the bundle of Michael's clothes (with the local meaning of *difficult* or *evil*), and as his body floated to the far north, there was no one to keen him but the sea birds, the "black hags that do be flying on the sea." There is nothing remarkable about Synge's use of black to suggest ideas of evil and death, but when Michael's grave rope is taken by Bartley to ride to the sea upon the mare, the prophetic im-plication is given particular color by the fact that the pig with black feet had been eating it—a pig destined itself for death and the jobber.

A recurrent pattern of superimposed events also widens the horizon of the play and establishes the sense of repetition, of the closing circle of death in the world of the play. In this function the figure of the drowned Michael dominates the opening of the play and persists as a presence among the characters. He is not only a part of Maurya's vision but also a reminder of the ruthlessness of the sea; he becomes *present* through the bundle of his clothing the priest has brought. "And isn't it a pitiful thing when there is nothing left of a man who was a great rower and fisher but a bit of an old shirt and a plain stocking?" His identity is established, but he is also a general symbol for all the drowned men of the sea: "There does be a power of young men floating round in the sea, and what way would they know if it was Michael they had, or another man like him, for when a man is nine days in the sea, and the wind blowing, it's hard set his own mother would be to say what man was in it." As the girls discover, Michael's shirt is worn by Bartley as he rides to his death, for his own had been that morning prophetically made "heavy with the salt in it." And it is a stick Michael has brought to the house that Maurya takes to lean on as she makes her painful journey to the spring well to give Bartley his bit of bread. This seems to Maurya a violation of the natural order ("In the big world the old people /50/ do be leaving things after them for their sons. . . ."), a violation which is natural— typical, at least—on the island, where the words of the priest are simply not relevant, based as they are on a vision of a world in which what is "natural" is also that which is just. "It's little the like of him knows of the sea."

The pattern of repetition builds in intensity as the play approaches its conclusion, for, in a wonderfully effective scene, Synge gives us Maurya telling of the deaths of all the men of the family. As she describes the neighbors bringing in Patch in "the half of a red sail, and water dripping out of it," Bartley, who had been then a baby lying on her knees, is carried in: "They're carrying a thing among them, and there's water dripping out of it and leaving a track by the big stones." Childhood to manhood to death: the cycle of life is fulfilled, and nothing remains but acceptance and cessation from struggle. Michael's coffin boards will do as well for Bartley. The only wonder is that Maurya has forgotten the coffin nails.

The neighbors who bring in Bartley's body move with sure familiarity, performing the necessary and familiar tasks; and with the keening women and the kneeling men, the sense of the community of death among the islanders is firmly established. The keen is a formalized expression of grief, pagan in origin, choral in function. By ritual, pagan and Christian, by formalizing grief, death is endured; and the conclusion of *Riders to the Sea* is reminiscent in many respects of the graveyard scenes of *The Aran Islands,* in which Christian prayer follows the keening for the dead: "There was an irony in these words of atonement and Catholic belief spoken by voices that were still hoarse with the cries of pagan desperation." Irony is not the right word to apply to the effect of the conclusion of *Riders to the Sea,* although for Synge it may have been present in the undifferentiated use of pagan and Christian ritual; the rituals are equally ineffectual in *changing* this universe, but they do enable man to endure it. The ritualized ending of the play has the effect of the formal, concluding speech of Greek or Renaissance drama; and it contributes to the sense of impersonal, "ritual" tragedy which the play gives.

Although Maurya is the central figure of the play, the tragedy is nonetheless largely external in its presentation, objective in its lack of personal emphasis. The antagonist is the sea, an /51/ unseen but very real presence; and Maurya as protagonist is "like a type of the women's life on the islands" more than she is a personally realized character. Attention is focused upon Maurya from the beginning of the play; the speeches of the two girls, even before she appears, show a concern for her reactions rather than for their own. It is also her reaction to the death of Bartley rather than his death *per se* which is the (muted) surprise of the play, for she is able in the end of the play to answer her earlier question to Bartley: "What way will I live and the girls with me, and I an old woman looking for the grave?" Her conflict with Bartley, her attempt to keep him from going on the sea, points up the deeper conflict between the cottage and the sea, for "It's the life of a young man to be going on the sea," although as Maurya knows, death is the necessary outcome of such a life. There is an unpretentious heroism in these people and their struggle with the sea.

II Poetry of the Theater

Part of Synge's achievement is to make the reader and the audience aware that the action of this brief moment of his play takes place on the last day of a long struggle—stretching literally over generations— that the mother has waged with the sea; and he has done this by creating an intensity which pushes back the limits imposed by the brevity of the play. The play moves with an intensity which can only be achieved by poetic means, and although *Riders to the Sea* is not technically poetic drama, it is one of the finest of twentieth-century examples of poetry of the theater (to be distinguished, in Cocteau's

terms, from poetry *in* the theater). The rhythmic language of the
play, while not in "verse" lines, adds to the total effect of the play—
much more effectively, in fact, than the verse in many verse dramas.
There is an appropriate austerity in the language and rhythmic
speech of the characters, as well as an effective mingling of innocence
and muted awe before the fate which has the family so firmly in its
grasp. The speeches of Maurya—particularly the longer speeches in
the concluding moments of the play—have a formal quality as she
recounts, almost ritualistically, the triumphs of fate and the losses
of man.

A comparison of *Riders to the Sea* with *Blood Wedding*, a /52/
consciously poetic drama by the Spanish poet García Lorca, under-
scores the poetic nature of Synge's play. *Blood Wedding* invites comparison, for it is, like *Riders to the Sea*, a folk tragedy and a tragedy
of fate.[2] It is also, however, a play which, like *Riders to the Sea*,
transcends its origin in folk tragedy to make a large universal statement. The situations are similar also; in both plays there is the death
of a male line as the result of the unyielding demands of fate,
although the Lorca play (written thirty years after *Riders to the Sea*)
is more complex and not so single in its effect as the Synge play, a
complexity which is reflected in the multiplicity of theatrical tech-
niques and poetic devices which Lorca uses in his tragedy of three
acts and seven scenes. Yet the effect is the same as that of the one-act,
one-scene play by Synge, and the conclusions of the two plays have
a similar quality. In both plays the women endure; the necessary
demands of life and manhood have caused the death of the men of
the families in the irresistible working out of a struggle begun long
before the opening curtain of either play. The neighbors are used in
both plays to establish the community implications of the tragedies;
and Lorca, who uses colors as persistently for symbolic meaning as
Synge in *Riders to the Sea*, opens his final scene with two girls wind-
ing a red skein, an effect which serves the same comment as the similar symbolic elements in the Synge play.

Riders to the Sea is no more a static drama than is *Blood Wedding*,
a notion which has persisted even in the opinion of John Gassner, one
of the finest modern critics of drama. "The play is truly, profoundly
'static drama,' the theory for which was laid down by another 'symbol-

---

[2] This rather inevitable comparison has been made in an essay I have not been
able to see: Patrick O. Dudgeon, "J. M. Synge and Federico Garcia Lorca,"
Fantasy, No. 26 (1942).

ist' successor of Baudelaire, Verlaine, Rimbaud, and other *decadents*, Maurice Maeterlinck."[3] *Riders to the Sea*, according to Gassner, lacks the active engagement of the characters in their tragic fates, which one finds, for example, in Sophocles' *Oedipus*. Synge was reading Maeterlinck, it is true, even during his first visit to the Aran Islands, and he wrote a review of *La Sagesse et la Destinée* for *The Daily Express* of Dublin in December of 1898, which indicated his interest in Maeterlinck. But later, in thinking aloud in his notebooks, Synge rejects the idea of drama which Maeterlinck represents: "There is always the poet's dream which makes itself a sort of world, where it is kept a dream. Is this possible on /53/ the stage? I think not. Maeterlinck, *Pelléas and Mélisande?* Is the drama as a beautiful thing a lost art? . . . For the present the only possible beauty in drama is peasant drama. For the future we must await the making of life beautiful again before we can have beautiful drama."[4] Synge is, of course, dealing here with beauty on the stage; but, as always, the reality necessary to true beauty is implicit, and he rejects the ideas behind Maeterlinck's kind of drama, which can exist only in the "poet's dream."

Synge's dislike of Yeats' *The Shadowy Waters*, which may well be described as "Symbolist" or "static" drama, is expressed in correspondence with his friend, Stephen MacKenna,[5] roughly in the period of the staging of *Riders to the Sea*; and it seems most likely that Synge for one would have objected to a description of his play which would have placed it in the same category as *The Shadowy Waters*. In Yeats' play and in *Pelléas*, for example—plays which *are* "static drama"—there is indeed absence of the sense of active engagement; the effect is one of dream, of a fixed, unreal picture in which the playwright is concerned with the adornment of his scene rather than with its conflict.

Riders to the Sea gives an entirely different impression, although it is not possible to locate the action within the psychology of character, which is what Gassner seems to refer to when he compares *Riders to the Sea* with *Oedipus*. The conflict in Synge's play is a conflict with the sea, which is not, as in *The Shadowy Waters*, simply the element the characters drift upon. The sea is, instead, the antagonist— as unyielding as fate; indeed, it is the agent of fate in the play. The sea is not merely a part of a tapestry-like background as in *The*

---

[3] *The Theatre in Our Times* (New York, 1954), p. 3.
[4] David H. Greene and Edward M. Stephens, *J. M. Synge, 1871–1909* (New York, 1959), p. 259.
[5] *Ibid.*, p. 157.

Shadowy Waters; it enters into the small cottage in every speech, in the clothes of the drowned man, in Maurya's fears for Bartley, and in every memory of the past, a past defined by the sea. A choice is made in the play which engages the will of the characters—the decision of Bartley to make his fateful journey upon the sea, a decision which is only a part of the larger choice made by all the men of the islands. And the women participate in this destiny and express their participation in the manner in which they face their engulfing enemy. The struggle between Maurya and Bartley is certainly not a static thing, and it becomes a micro- /54/ cosmic expression of the larger struggle—the contest between the cottage and the sea. There is also in the Synge play a strong sense of intensely real human *engagement*, of human commitment which exists on a level usually not the concern of the "Symbolist" drama. There are ways of behaving, rules for existence to which man is obligated even if the contest with the sea is an uneven and a hopeless one. Although she cannot dissuade him from his going, Maurya's obligation to the unheeding Bartley is expressed in her painful journey to the spring well, bearing his bit of bread and a blessing. The fact that she is thwarted by her vision does not deny the sense of human obligation which is everywhere strongly expressed in the play—a play which is more nearly modern in its outlook and presentation than Symbolist and more *active* than static, although the activity is not in accord with a modern preference for a psychologically centered activity.

Denis Johnston

Riders to the Sea*

* * *

/18/ There are still a few old people on the Aran Islands who remember Synge, and many more who are prepared to repeat what they heard about him from their elders. Probably the most significant tribute that can be paid to his memory is the fact that on the whole they speak well of him—which is more than can be said for another visitor, Robert Flaherty, the film director, whose sentimental enthusiasms for everything about the islanders would appear at first blush to be more flattering to the ego than Synge's sardonic understanding. But however flattering it may seem, no community enjoys being pressed to assume the clothes and practices of fifty years ago for the purpose of making it seem more picturesque than it is today. Aran men do not wear funny tam-o-shanters, nor attempt to harpoon sun-fish, nor fish off the top of the cliffs of Dun Aengus, and they see no point—apart from a financial one—in pretending that they do. On the other hand, *Riders to the Sea* may not be quite the sort of play that a man from Kilmurvy would write about his family, but there are many things in it that he understands. Above all, he appreciates the fact that it does not insist that he is picturesque.

The Greek analogy is legitimate here. *Riders to the Sea* has a classical unity and a completeness that makes one aware of the fact that in a sense it has ended before it begins. What happens is inevitable, and in this fact resides the real nub of its tragedy. There is no need for us to make up our minds whether or not we like the doomed

* Reprinted from *John Millington Synge*. New York and London: Columbia University Press, 1965, pp. 18-23, by permission of the publisher. © 1965 by Columbia University Press.

Bartley, or even whether we are at all sorry for his predecessor, Michael, whose clothes are laid out on the table. It is not Bartley's death over which we grieve, nor even the death of Man. Everybody must die sooner or later—a fact which, as a rule, is a matter for congratulation rather than the reverse. "Sooner or later" is the operative part of the statement here, and the pity of the play is that in this community the young tend to go before the old.

> In the big world, says Maurya, the old people do be leaving things /19/ after them for their sons and children, but in this place it is the young men do be leaving things behind for them that do be old.

Riders is probably the most frequently performed of all Synge's plays—principally by amateurs, and most frequently of all in schools and colleges. It appears to present no difficulties in casting, and the sentiments to which it gives voice do not seem to offer any obvious problems either in interpretation or direction. That it does not usually manage to convey the required sensation of catharsis but merely one of depression is probably owing to the fact that both these impressions are wrong—usually as wrong as the costuming.

Riders to the Sea is not a play about a tiresome community that insists on going on with its fishing in spite of inadequate equipment and a continuing disregard for the weather reports. It is true that one son after another gets drowned, and it is not difficult to experience a certain mild irritation with Bartley—the baby of the family—who continues to wave aside all warnings, until he finishes up precisely where one would expect to find him—laid out on the table. And then one has to put up with an outburst of passionate mourning with which the performance usually ends. Without a suggestion of suspense, or some illumination of character or motivation, it is usually a pleasure when it is over. And one asks oneself how can such an expression of the obvious be put in the category of the great—except as some formal gesture of respect for peasants, for Ireland, and for Synge?

The point is, of course, that *Riders to the Sea* is a much better play than this kind of treatment suggests, and is far from easy either to cast or to perform. A superficial production of the type that has been mentioned has nothing to do with the classical form, but makes it instead into an inadequate Faust story, in which the victim goes to his predicted fate without ever having had an evening of love in return for his pains. On this basis, it would be a very much better play if Bartley were not going to the mainland to sell horses but to savor the stews /20/ of that sophisticated Babylon, the city of Galway. This would certainly give it something of the pious Christian touch that, prior to Goethe, was a necessity to any Faust story. If the production suggests that a matter of free choice is involved, and that Bartley goes on in spite of the warnings that a more sensible son would observe, it can be nothing but a Faust story. Yet whoever heard of a Faust who barters his future to attend a horse fair?

But *Riders to the Sea* is neither pious nor basically Christian. It is Orestean, and in the true Greek tradition, where no moral choice at all is offered to the characters. The sea—not the Gods—is the source of the law in this play, and there is no escape from it. The play is not trying to tell us how sad it is to have a son drowned—especially if he happens to be the last. We might be expected to know this already, and no play, classical or otherwise, can be great if it merely tells us something that we have expected from the start, without even an element of surprise in the telling.

What the play does tell us is the effect of the inevitable on these people, and what, if anything, man's answer to the Gods should be. In order to appreciate the point of the last two pages it is necessary to understand two or three unmelodramatic and very Synge-like assumptions: first, that there is no moral element whatever involved in these people pursuing the life that is theirs, whether or not it must end in death. All life ends in death, and one does not say to a dying man, "There you are, now. This is what you get for having been born. I told you so, but you wouldn't listen." This is a correct Faust conclusion—and it is a fatuous one without an afterlife in either heaven or hell. But nobody has any data on Bartley's final destination. The play is about him being drowned—not about his character. So it is clearly the gods whom we are up against—not a moral judgment.

The dilemma is that of Orestes, who by the law of life is /21/ bound to avenge his father. But by the law of life he must not kill his mother. What is he to do, except protest against the law of life?

So, also, Bartley must go down to the sea, and if in doing so he meets his end, there is no element of "I told you so" about it. His mother must accept the situation. But there is an answer that she may give, an answer that is the point of the play.

> They're all gone now [she says], and there isn't anything more that the sea can do to me . . . I'll have no call now to be crying and praying when the wind breaks from the south, and you can hear the surf is in the east, and the surf is in the west, making a great stir with the two noises, and they hitting one on the other. I'll have no call now to be going down and getting Holy Water in the dark nights after Samhain, and I wont care what way the sea is when the other women will be keening . . . it's a great rest I'll have now, and it's time, surely. It's a

great rest I'll have now, and great sleeping in the long nights after Samhain, if it's only a bit of wet flour we do have to eat, and maybe a fish that would be stinking.

These expressions of human dignity under the buffetings of life are not wails of anguish, nor are they even projections of the stoicism of Job. They are man's answer to Heaven, and should be played as such. They give tongue to much the same idea that is to be found in a minor key in *Waiting for Godot,* where Vladimir protests

> . . . we are blessed in this, that we happen to know the answer. Yes, in this immense confusion one thing alone is clear. We are waiting for Godot to come—or for night to fall. We have kept our appointment and that's an end to that. We are not saints, but we have kept our appointment. How many people can boast as much?

This is a universal answer, the significance of which we are finding extremely pertinent since the coming of the Atomic Age. Yet here it is expressed in 1903. But there is also a more special element that Synge dramatizes in the course of the play which also contains great theatrical possibilities. Bartley is drowned, but this is not by chance. He does not fall casually /22/ into the water, nor does he go down with some ship. It is the rearing of the horse behind that knocks him off the cliff. And who is riding on the rearmost horse? The ghost of his brother Michael.

Here we notice another important element of the folk attitude toward the dead themselves. In some ways it resembles the popular attitude toward the fairies that is so vividly underlined in *Heart's Desire.* In Irish eyes the fairies are not Shakespearean or Gilbertean creatures,

> Tripping hither, tripping thither,
> Nobody knows why or whither.

They are malevolent beings who steal children away with specious promises of better times. So, too, the dead want company. It is the ghostly Michael who is the killer of his younger brother—for reasons that lie deep in the Irish psychology, and are the basis of a universal fear of the dead. Count Dracula presents us with a vulgarized version of the same idea; but debased or not, the story is the same: in the half-world of the grave, there is a host of conjured spirits who would, if they could, make us like themselves.

That the dead are not to be trusted is an idea to be found even in that most sinister of spiritualistic farces—*Blithe Spirit* by Noel Coward. In Synge's play the sea is the executioner, but the horses

make the occasion—the horses that must be sold at the fair but that
carry the dead no less than the living. Herein we find that union of
causation and denouement that is the sure sign of a well-constructed
play. There is no escape, owing to the fact that the Urge is its own
Consequence.

The play is misinterpreted if it ends in a screaming match of com-
petitive grief—or indeed in a performance that suggests stoic indifference.

> Bartley will have a fine coffin out of the white boards, and a deep grave
> surely. What more can we want than that? No man at all can be living
> for ever, and we must be satisfied. /23/

The priest is not right when he says

> . . . she'll be getting her death with crying and lamenting . . . Herself
> does be saying prayers half through the night, and the Almighty God
> won't leave her destitute.

God does leave her destitute. And it is her own dead who bring it
about—a double blow to which she gives the only answer, even though
nobody listens.

> It's the life of a young man to be going on the sea, and who would listen
> to an old woman with one thing, and she saying it over?

Riders to the Sea is hard to cast, and needs to be very subtly inter-
preted; otherwise it is liable to appear as a dreary little suspense
story without any suspense.

Paul M. Levitt

The Structural Craftsmanship of
J. M. Synge's *Riders to the Sea**

Riders to the Sea is of considerable technical interest because of the
methods by which Synge obtained intensity and compression within a
single act. So clearly did Synge insinuate early in the play a subsequent course of action, that there can be no doubt how the play will
end. Indeed, Synge's successful communication of the inevitability of
an early death for the fishermen of the Aran Islands has frequently
been commented on. Charles Tennyson observes that "in *Riders to the
Sea* . . . the interest is not that of doubt. . . . The certainty [of Bartley's
death] is so great that there is hardly even the interest of suspense."[1]
This verdict is echoed by Ernest Boyd,[2] Percival Wilde,[3] Alan Price,[4]
and others. However, in none of these discussions is there any attempt
to see how the imagery and the structure of the action extend the
borders, and hence the meaning, of the play to create a sense of fate
and timeless repetition.

The major thematic strain of recurring death is initiated in the title
of the play and is maintained through allusions to the books of
Exodus and Revelation. The biblical allusions combine not only
literary levels, but also temporal levels: they bring together past,
present, and future in a continuum of NOW. The title *Riders to the
Sea* alludes to the /54/ fatal ride in Exodus by Pharaoh's horsemen

* Reprinted from *Eire-Ireland*, IV (Spring, 1969), 53-61, by permission of the
author and the journal.
1 Charles Tennyson, "Irish Plays and Playwrights," *The Quarterly Review*,
ccxv (July, 1911), 231.
2 Ernest Boyd, *The Contemporary Drama of Ireland* (Boston, 1917), p. 96.
3 Percival Wilde, *The Craftsmanship of the One-Act Play* (Boston, 1926), p. 64.
4 Alan Price, *Synge and Anglo-Irish Drama* (London, 1961), p. 188.

who pursued the Israelites to the midst of the sea and, in consequence, suffered the Lord's wrath for their disobedience. ("Then sang Moses and the children of Israel this song unto the Lord, and spake, saying, I will sing unto the Lord, for he hath triumphed gloriously: the horse and his rider hath he thrown into the sea" [Ex. 15:1].) [5] In particular, the title applies to Michael and Bartley, the two sons of Maurya's who figure in the play, and upon whom Maurya's vision centers. Synge gives to all the drowned fishermen of the Aran Islands, including all the men in Maurya's family, the fate associated with Pharaoh's horsemen. He thus expands the dimensions of the tragedy and gives the play universality.

However, Synge is even more indebted to the Revelation of Saint John the Divine than to Exodus for the imagery and allusions in *Riders.* The revelation purports to be the revelation of Jesus Christ to His servant John in Patmos "to shew . . . things which must shortly come to pass" (Rev. 1:1). It sums up the theme of earthly mortality present in both testaments, while developing, among other things, the Alpha and Omega metaphor—the end of life on earth and the beginning of the life to come. *Riders,* too, concerns the Alpha and Omega of life. And as well, *Riders* has a vision of the future (and also memories of death in the past), and an overall plan which shows "things which must shortly come to pass."

The impression of an unbroken cycle of death inevitably working itself out is a direct result of the organization in the play. By interweaving the elements of the action in such a way as to suggest the presence of a fatal nexus binding each male member of the family to the next, Synge captures the timeless rhythm of recurring death. Through the figures of the two horsemen—Michael and Bartley—/55/ are symbolically represented the death of the first rider in the past and the death of the last rider in the present. The riders to the sea are the beginning and the ending, the first and the last riders, victims of the relentless repetition of the eternal pattern.

---

[5] Synge's biographers, David H. Green and Edward M. Stephens, discuss the thoroughness of Synge's religious upbringing and his mother's orthodoxy in the first chapter of *J. M. Synge: 1871–1909* (New York, 1959). Worth quoting here is the following passage: "Except for . . . four years of irregular schooling, all of [Synge's] education until he enrolled at Trinty College, Dublin, was at the hands of a private tutor whom he saw three times a week in his own home. But there was nothing irregular or haphazard about his religious training, for his mother and grandmother ruled a household where the discipline was almost as strict as that of a religious order. Mrs. Synge and her mother had gone to school themselves to a harsh master. Their authority was the Bible, and they cited it constantly to all the children" (p. 7).

The play begins as the tragedy, begun many years before, nears completion. Four sons, a husband, and a husband's father have already drowned. There is fear that a fifth son (Michael) has drowned, and that the sixth son (Bartley), the last, is readying himself to go down to the sea. The exposition establishes the relationship between those who have died in the past and those who will die shortly. The present action portrays Nora and Cathleen's concern to identify "a shirt and a plain stocking [that] were got off a drowned man in Donegal" in order to determine if they are Michael's, and the concern of all three women—Maurya and her daughters, Nora and Cathleen—as to whether or not Bartley will leave.

Thus, the lines along which this tragedy of fate will proceed are clear. While we anxiously wait for the completion of an event (Michael's journey) which began before the play opened, we are witness to the start of a new event (Bartley's forthcoming trip). The first event is sustained long enough to permit the second event to begin. This organization contributes to the sense of an inexorable fate, because the overlapping actions proclaim the relatedness of both events. Even as Bartley is preparing to journey to the sea, we suspect that his passage is a renewal of Michael's passage, as Michael's was a renewal of the journeys of the men who preceded him. The very nature of the pattern seems to demand that Bartley must die too.

Bartley's fate, which we have guessed at all along, is first realized, symbolically, in his exit speech:

Bartley (taking the halter.) I must go now quickly. I'll ride down on the red mare, and the gray pony'll run behind me. . . . The blessing of God on you. (He goes out.)

Those familiar with the Apocalypse will have a presentiment of tragedy, knowing that the red mare and the gray pony invoke the memory of the Four Horsemen (Rev. 6:1–8). The apocalyptic symbolism here at once reinforces the biblical imagery of the title and focuses attention on Bartley's exit, emphasizing the likelihood of his dying. Moreover, not only does the apocalyptic symbolism foreshadow /56/ the death of Bartley at the end of the play, but it also prepares us for the continuation and development of that symbolism in Maurya's dream.

Shortly after Bartley has gone, Maurya leaves to overtake him in order to give him the bread which the girls have baked for his trip. At this point, Synge returns the action to the question of Michael's fate, that is, to the identification of the clothing. By doing so, he emphasizes through the very organization of the play the theme of a beginning-to-end cycle relentlessly and fatally working itself out in the deaths of Maurya's sons and husband and husband's father. To begin the second action, Bartley's departure, before the first action, the identification of Michael's clothes, is concluded, gives the impression of the separate actions being related.[6]

As Maurya returns from looking for Bartley, she enters slowly, in silence. She is still holding the bread. We sense that Maurya's weary and reticent entrance is the result of her having missed Bartley. We would little suspect that it is because she *has seen* Bartley. Consequently, almost half the scene is played ironically, because it is played under the assumption that Maurya's depression is the result of her unsuccessful attempt to intercept Bartley. Her eventual revelation, therefore, is doubly effective, revealing at once the irony of her having in fact seen Bartley and the vision which is at the heart of the play's meaning.

Cathleen breaks the silence, asking, "You didn't give him his bit of bread?" But Maurya does not answer. Instead, there is a stage direction which tells us that "Maurya begins to keen softly, without turning round." The bread has gone undelivered; Maurya has not made contact with Bartley. In all times, bread has been equated with life and the living. The important allusion here is that of coming for- /57/ ward, making contact, receiving the bread. To fail to make contact is, symbolically, to die.

Maurya reveals that she has seen "Michael himself." To which Cathleen answers: "You did not, mother; it wasn't Michael you seen, for his body is after being found in the far north, and he's got a clean burial by the grace of God." But Maurya is not to be put off, and Cathleen's contradiction only urges her to a complete revelation of what it is she has seen:

> Maurya [a little defiantly]. I'm after seeing him this day, and he riding and galloping. Bartley came first on the red mare; and I tried to say "God speed you," but something choked the words in my throat. He went by quickly; and "the blessing of God on you," says he, and I could

---

[6] Synge was also obliged for dramatic reasons to begin a second action before he could resolve the first. Not to have overlapped the actions would have created a "dead spot" following the resolution of the Michael question, which in turn would have compelled Synge to find "something" to occupy the stage from the time that Michael's death is discovered until the time Bartley's subsequent death is known. (Not many plays can stand such "dead spots," and especially not a one-act play.) Synge does not permit any relaxation of tension or interest; the Michael question sustains the suspense until the Bartley question is reintroduced. For a similar comment on this scene, see: Kenneth Thorpe Rowe, *Write That Play* (New York, 1939), p. 103.

say nothing. I looked up then, and I crying, at the gray pony, and there
was Michael upon it—with fine clothes on him, and new shoes on his
feet.

What Maurya has seen is, apocalyptically, the end of Michael and
Bartley's life on earth. (And certainly nowhere is the imagery of
Revelation more evident than in Maurya's vision.) The allusion under-
lying her vision reinforces the idea of a terrible destiny being visited
upon the men in her family. We are uneasy upon hearing what it is
that Maurya has seen, remembering the red horse and the gray (pale)
horse Bartley and Michael ride and the fine clothes and new shoes
that Michael's phantasm wears. For the red and gray ponies remind
us of the Four Horsemen—and death. Michael's fine clothes remind
us of the new linen in Revelation: "And to [the righteous] was
granted that [they] should be arrayed in fine linen, clean and white:
for the fine linen is the righteousness of saints" (Rev. 19:8). "And
the armies *which were* in heaven followed [the Word of God] upon
white horses, clothed in fine linen, white and clean" (Rev. 19:14).
What Maurya has seen is a vision of death and the promise of the
life to come. The horses Michael and Bartley ride symbolize the
brothers' deaths, and Michael's new clothes his life to come. In terms
of the dramatic action, Michael and Bartley represent the Alpha and
Omega of male life in their family. (The "first" of Maurya's last
two remaining sons, Michael, has already concluded his fatal ride as
the last son, Bartley, is beginning his.) By dramatizing only the final
steps in the fatal pattern, Synge is letting the part stand for the
whole. /58/ The Michael and Bartley action represents in small the
larger cycle of mortality which has taken the lives of eight men.
Moreover, Synge emphasizes the chronology of this cycle by having
the "first" son (Michael) dressed in fine clothes and the last son
(Bartley) not. This is to indicate in time that Michael is already
dead, but Bartley has not died yet, although fated to die.

Hence, Maurya's vision is completely functional; it serves to secure
the imagery and meaning in the play and to implement the theme.
The figure of the red and gray horses reinforces the timelessness of
Michael's and Bartley's ride and the meaning of the play's title; it
introduces the richness of the death imagery in Revelation, while the
mention of "fine clothes" suggests the salvation of the righteous.

Expanding and extending the significance of Maurya's vision and
the theme of an inexorable fate, Synge, in what is perhaps the finest
touch in the play, dramatizes the idea of recurrent death by repeating
in the background (of the stage) in pantomime the dreadful home-
coming pageant which Maurya is describing in the foreground. At

the same time that Maurya is recounting the men who have passed from her to death and the scenes of their dying and their homecoming, a similar scene (a "ghost scene") is reenacted in silence, as the towns-people, bearing the dead Bartley,[7] enter noiselessly in the back-ground.

> Maurya. . . . There were Stephen, and Shawn, were lost in the great wind, and found after in the Bay of Gregory of the Golden Mouth, and carried up the two of them on the one plank, and in by that door.
> [She pauses for a moment, the girls start as if they heard something through the door that is half open behind them.]
> Nora (in a whisper). Did you hear that, Cathleen? Did you hear a noise in the north-east? /59/
> Cathleen (in a whisper). There's some one after crying out by the seashore.
> Maurya (continues without hearing anything). There was Sheamus and his father, and his own father again, were lost in a dark night, and not a stick or sign was seen of them when the sun went up. There was Patch after was drowned out of a curragh that turned over. I was sitting here with Bartley, and he a baby, lying on my two knees, and I seen two women, and three women, and four women coming in, and they crossing themselves, and not saying a word. I looked out then, and there were men coming after them, and they holding a thing in the half of a red sail, and water dripping out of it—it was a dry day, Nora—and leaving a track to the door.
> [She pauses again with her hand stretched out toward the door. It opens softly and old women begin to come in, crossing themselves on the threshold, and kneeling down in front of the stage with red petti-coats over their heads.][8]

---

7 Notwithstanding Synge's efforts to permit enough time for Bartley's death to occur, we know, as L. A. G. Strong says, that "a very few (terrestrial) minutes pass between Bartley's departure and the entry of the neighbours bearing his dead body: certainly not enough for all to happen off the stage which we are told happened." If there is something of a time problem here, we are inclined to ignore it. Time being as short as it is in a one-act play, we make allowances for what in fact could not occur, but does. Furthermore, as Strong goes on to point out, "so skillfully do we push forward to learn what has happened, that we never think of the time measured by the watch on our wrist or in our waistcoat pocket. Such a play as *Riders to the Sea* takes us out of time altogether." (L. A. G. Strong, *Common Sense About Drama* [New York, 1937], p. 53).

8 Alan Price sees this scene as summing up the whole range of tragedy represented in the play. "The enactment on the stage," writes Price ". . . is the climax to Maurya's words, a concrete example to reinforce them, and also a symbolic representation of all the deaths on the island, and elsewhere. It hardly matters whether it is Patch or Michael or Bartley that is being brought home: all at some time or other find alike the inevitable end, and the one ritual we see on the stage is not only for Bartley but for all of them. Everything combines to persuade spectators that they are watching a scene of universal significance." (Alan Price, *Synge and Anglo-Irish Drama* [London, 1961], p. 188).

Maurya's speech by itself is a testament to a life of suffering, recalled at a prophetic moment of sheer hopelessness. Furthermore, by means of the pantomime, Synge captures the ritualistic significance of death and creates a fugal quality in the whole play. It is here that Synge finally harvests the labor of constructing a pattern of repetitive action in which background, theme, and language are repeatedly interwoven.

Throughout the play Synge has been emphasizing the inevitability of premature and violent death suffered by the Aran islanders. The background of a relentless and formidable sea has been particularly influential in persuading us to this idea. In addition, Synge's language reinforces the theme and mood. Almost chant-like, the redundant cadences of Synge's prose seem to duplicate the awful regularity of the sea and the keening of the women.

In the final speeches of the play, Synge again returns to the idea of /60/ an unalterable fate which links Maurya's dead. He gains the effect of concatenated deaths by repeating the news of Michael's death and, at the same time, revealing Bartley's death. While handing Maurya the few recovered pieces of Michael's clothing, Cathleen explains to her that they were found in the far north. Then in the next speech, Nora, in a most dehumanizing description tells how the dead Bartley is come home: a speech which echoes Maurya's description of a moment before in the pantomime scene, of how Patch's drowned body was carried into the house. "They're carrying a thing among them and there's water dripping out of it and leaving a track by the big stones." Maurya's, Cathleen's, and Nora's speeches, following one after another, as they do, give the effect of being related. Bartley's death is confirmed when Cathleen, almost too afraid to ask what she already knows, whispers, "Is it Bartley it is?" Without even hearing the reply of "one of the women"—"It is surely, God rest his soul"—we know that the dread cycle is completed.

As Bartley is brought in, Cathleen asks how he was drowned. This is important because the reply to her question by one of the women— "The gray pony knocked him into the sea, and he was washed out where there is a great surf on the white rocks"—brings us back to the symbolism of the horses in Revelation. But it is to be remembered that Bartley was riding the red mare, which means that the gray pony caused Bartley to be thrown from his own horse into the sea below. It is fitting that when Bartley dies, his death is caused by the gray pony, the horse specifically associated with death. ("And I looked, and behold a pale horse: and his name that sat on him was Death" [Rev. 6:8].) Also, it is meaningful that Bartley's death resulted from his having been thrown into the sea, because if we remember from

Exodus that "the horse and his rider hath [the Lord] thrown into the sea," and the analogue to be found in the meaning of the title, *Riders to the Sea*, we are reminded by both that being thrown into the sea is equated with death.

Furthermore, "the white rocks" to which Bartley's body was carried by the surf are the same ones that Cathleen has mentioned earlier in the play in conjunction with a stormy sea. Cathleen asks: "Is the sea bad by the white rocks, Nora?" By alerting us to the rocks early in the play (rocks associated with a bad sea), Synge foreshadows the place of Bartley's death. By mentioning the rocks a second time, Synge /61/ emphasizes the point that death is always close at hand and that it occurs in familiar places. Also, the double reference to the white rocks serves, in the overall design of the play, to introduce the threat of the sea and to summarize its symbolism. By significant repetition Synge links the beginning and ending of *Riders*, reinforcing our sense of the cyclical action operating in the play.

Briefly, then, in *Riders*, Synge captures the pattern of death by focusing on a point shortly before the end of the cycle, dramatizing only the last two deaths in the family—those of Michael and Bartley. In this way, and by careful exposition, he compresses past and present action into the closing moments of a tragedy long unfolding. It is this organization, combined with the biblical imagery in the play, which gives *Riders* its extraordinary compactness and intensity, making of the prior drownings and the present tragedy one unbroken action.

Robin Skelton

Introduction to *Riders to the Sea**

* * *

Riders to the Sea has, like many works of Art, suffered somewhat
from its popularity and from the activities of those critics who, faced
with anything relating to the Irish peasantry, turn immediately into
pseudo-sociologists, philologists, and Irish patriots. It is as absurd to
regard this play as a play of merely regional interest as it would be to
regard *Cymbeline* as a study of Roman Britain. Great drama escapes
its locale and its time. Nevertheless, in reading the play those who
have any knowledge at all of Irish drama will be forced to recall an
earlier play by W. B. Yeats in which there are certain parallels to
Synge's play. *Cathleen ni Houlihan* was first produced by W. G. Fay's
Irish National Dramatic Company at St. Teresa's Hall, Clarendon
Street, Dublin in 1902 on April 2, 3, and 4. The lyrics from it were
published in *The United Irishman* on April 15th. The play itself
was published in *Samhain*, and as a book in October of the same year.

Synge's earliest notes for *Riders to the Sea* cannot be dated with
any certainty. His first extended attempt at the play however has
been dated by Dr. Saddlemyer as belonging to the period Spring-
Summer 1902. It seems, therefore, that Synge was writing *Riders to
the Sea* with *Cathleen ni Houlihan* fresh in his mind.

The parallels between the two plays are not excessive, but they are
interesting. Both plays are set in a cottage; both plays begin with a
question; the protagonists in both plays /20/ introduce the main

* Reprinted from J. M. Synge, *Riders to the Sea*, edited by Robin Skelton from
the manuscript in the Houghton Library in Harvard University, with five lino
cuts in colour by Tate Adams, Dolmen Editions IX. Dublin: The Dolmen Press,
1969, pp. 19-33, by permission of the publisher. © 1969 by The Dolmen Press.

action by an examination of clothing; the old woman in both plays devotes much time to a rhetorical catalogue of the deaths of men attached to her; the young man whose immediate fate is the first concern of the play is in both cases called Michael; both plays end with the reexamination of the clothing involved.

These would be trivial parallels were it not that they were accompanied by mathematically precise contrasts. Yeats's Michael prepares for a wedding, and Synge's Michael for a funeral. Yeats's young men run down to the sea to join the French; Synge's Bartley goes down to the sea to travel to a horse-fair. The last words of Yeats's old woman imply a kind of immortality for the dead, for she sings:

> 'They shall be remembered for ever,
> They shall be alive for ever,
> They shall be speaking for ever.
> The people shall hear them for ever.'

Synge's old woman says, in the final words of the play, 'No man at all can be living for ever, and we must be satisfied.'

These contrasts and parallels are such as to suggest that Synge was, in some ways, reacting against Yeats.

Riders to the Sea is certainly a more universal drama than Yeats's play; the imagery of it is so organized as to refer us, not only to the world of Irish history and folklore, but also to the world of archetypal symbolism. It has been said that the sea is the main protagonist in the drama. An exchange early in the play juxtaposes references to the sea and to God:

> Nora . . . the Almighty God won't leave her destitute with no son living."
> Cailteen   Is the sea bad by the white rocks, Nora?
> Nora   Middling bad. God help us. /21/

The references to God in this play are, however, less precise than those to aspects of the landscape and the life of the characters. The points of the compass are used to emphasize the island-nature of the locale, but also for other reasons. Michael has been found in 'the far North'; the wind is 'rising in the south and west'. In the east, however, where the mainland lies, there may be hope for 'the tide's turning at the green head, and the hooker's tacking from the east' and it is from this direction that Maura believes Michael's body will come, rather than from the North. This emphasis upon the dominance of the sea makes the sea itself into a power, a god. One recalls the sea god,

Poseidon, for the death of Bartley is not unlike the death of Hippo-
litus. The latter had a more severe disagreement with Phaedra, of
course, but he certainly left the house without her blessing, having
rejected her incestuous love:

> Maura Isn't it a hard and cruel man, won't hear a word from an old
> woman, and she holding him from the sea?
> Cailteen It's the life of a young man to be going on the sea and who
> would listen to an old woman with one thing and she saying it over?
> Bartley I must go now quickly, I'll ride on the red mare, and the grey
> pony 'll run behind me. The blessing of God on you.
> Maura He's gone now, God spare us, and we'll not see him again. He's
> gone now, and when the black night is in it I'll have no son living in
> the world.
> Cailteen Why wouldn't you give him your blessing and he looking
> back in the door? Is n't sorrow enough is on every one in this house
> without your sending him out with an unlucky word behind him, and a
> hard word in his ear?

It was the 'hard word' of Phaedra that led to Theseus taking /22/ up
his option on the three wishes given him by Poseidon and causing the
horses of Hyppolitus to be startled by a sea-beast and his horse to
throw him to his death.

Synge has not done more than utilize the basic pattern of the myth;
he has made no explicit allusions. Nevertheless, the emphasis of the
play upon such design, and upon mythic feeling is clear. Every detail
contributes something. The pig with the black feet appears to be the
family's only asset. The pig is in mythology sacred both to the moon-
goddess (who rules the sea) and to the death-goddess, for it is an
eater of corpses. Swine in Irish mythology are thought to belong to
the Other World. Moreover it is Manannan mac Lir who instituted the
Faeth Fiadha at which the 'Pigs of Mannanan' are to be 'killed and
yet continue to exist for warriors'. Manannan Mac Lir is a god of the
sea.

The use of number is also significant in this play. Michael was missing for nine days. Maura, like Niobe, wept 'nine days' for her lost
son. Maura herself, recalling the drowning of Patch, reports that she
saw 'two women, and three women, and four women coming in'. This
adds up to nine again, as do the numbers mentioned by Bartley himself when he says optimistically 'you'll see me coming again in two
days, or in three days, or maybe in four days if the wind is bad.' Eight
men have been drowned of Maura's household: her husband's father,
her husband, and her six sons; the ninth death will, it is implied, be

Maura's own. The banquetting hall at Tara had nine chambers; these, it has been suggested, represented the eight main points of the compass and the central point.

The number nine is one familiar to all students of mythology. It is a triple trinity and therefore a potent number. An early draft of the play has Maura stating 'in three nights it is Martin's night'. Martinmas falls on November 11th so that /23/ the day of the play's action must be November 9th. November itself, is, as its name indicates, the ninth month of the ancient Roman calendar. Later versions of the play, however, suggest that the action takes place some time before Samhain, which is November Eve or Hallowe'en, the time when ghosts may walk and demons plague the earth, for Maura says, after the death of Bartley, 'I'll have no call to be going down and getting Holy Water in the dark nights after Samhain . . . It's a great rest I'll have now and great sleeping in the long nights after Samhain'.

Although the first complete draft of the play includes no nines, and no ghosts, the element of myth and superstition is still very much present. Martinmas is emphasized as a time of death (it is the slaughtering season). Patch says 'In three nights it is Martin's night and it is from this house a sheep must be killed'. In this version of the play Patch is drowned when he and another man 'were going after the hooker and he and another man leaned out to hit at them black birds with his oar, and when he did it a wave came behind them and upset them and it took Patch and washed him back by the rocks and he was drowned there.' These black birds can be identified from *The Aran Islands*; on page 181 of the Oxford Edition of the Collected Prose we read a story told Synge by an old man:

'Well, one Sunday a man came down and said there was a big ship coming into the sound. I ran down with two men and we went out in a curagh; we went round the point where they said the ship was, and there was no ship in it. As it was a Sunday we had nothing to do, and it was a fine calm day, so we rowed out a long way looking for the ship till I was further than I ever was before or after. When I wanted to turn back we saw a great flock of birds /24/ on the water and they all black, without a white bird through them. They had no fear of us at all, and the men with me wanted to go up to them, so we went further. When we were quite close they got up, so many that they blackened the sky, and they lit down again a hundred or maybe a hundred and twenty yards off. We went after them again, and one of the men wanted to kill one with the thole-pin, and the other man wanted to kill one with his rowing stick. I was afraid they would upset the curagh, but they would go after the birds.

When we were quite close one man threw the pin and the other man hit at them with his rowing stick, and the two of them fell over in the curagh, and she turned on her side and only it was quite calm the lot of us were drowned.

I think those black gulls and the ship were the same sort, and after that I never went out as a pilot. It is often curaghs go out to ships and find there is no ship.'

Although the black birds do not appear in the final version of the play, their use in the early version shows just how intent Synge was upon imbuing his play with mythic and supernatural feeling. In Irish legend supernatural beings often take the form of sea birds, and gulls are believed to be the souls of the drowned. The 'black birds' do not appear in the final version, of course, but there is a reference to 'the black hags that do be flying on the sea', and Bartley is on his way to see the ship when he is killed. In the paragraph immediately preceding the one I have just quoted we read another of the old man's stories:

'There do be strange things on the sea', he said. 'One night I was down there where you can see that green point, and I saw a ship coming in and I wondered what it would be doing coming so close to the rocks. It came straight /25/ on towards the place I was in, and then I got frightened and I ran to the houses, and when the captain saw me running he changed his course and went away.'

The implication here, of course, is that the ship was attempting to lure the man to his death, or maybe to a strange voyage. In *Riders to the Sea* Nora tells Cailteen that 'the tide's turning at the green head, and the hooker's tacking from the east.' A little later she says 'She's passing the green head, and letting fall her sails'.

Bartley's next speech is filled with dramatic irony:

I'll have half an hour to go down, and you'll see me coming again, in two days, or in three days, or maybe in four days if the wind is bad.

The death of Bartley is developed from several passages in *The Aran Islands*. The passage most usually regarded as important is that noted by Dr. Saddlemyer:

'When the horses were coming down to the slip an old woman saw her son, that was drowned a while ago, riding on one of them. She didn't say what she was after seeing, and this man caught the horse, he caught his own horse first, and then he caught this one, and after that he went out and was drowned. (p. 164)

Dr. Saddlemyer also refers to another story by the old man in which a young woman's ghost returns to her cottage to feed her child:

> 'She told them she was away with the fairies, and they could not keep her that night, though she was eating no food with the fairies, the way she might be able to come back to her child. Then she told them they would all be leaving that part of the country on the Oidhche Shamhna, /26/ and that there would be four or five hundred of them riding on horses, and herself would be on a grey horse, riding behind a young man. And she told them to go down to a bridge they would be crossing that night, and to wait at the head of it, and when she would be coming up she would slow the horse and they would be able to throw something on her and on the young man and they would fall over on the ground and be saved.' (p. 159)

There is a third passage which also relates to this theme of the traveller being followed by a ghost horse. The old man says:

> One night when he was coming home from the lighthouse he heard a man riding on the road behind him, and he stopped to wait for him, but nothing came. Then he heard as if there were a man trying to catch a horse on the rocks, and in a little time he went on. The noise behind him got bigger as he went along as if twenty horses and then as if a hundred or a thousand, were galloping after him. When he came to the stile where he had to leave the road and got over it, something hit against him and threw him down on the rock, and a gun he had in his hand fell into the field beyond him. (p. 180)

The notion of a large number of horses is associated with death by Maura when she says:

> If it was a hundred horses, or a thousand horses you had itself, what is the price of a thousand horses against a son where there is one son only?

It is worth noting that in the above stories the man escaped his fate once at a bridge and once at a stile; both bridges and stiles have many associations with faerie and the protection from faerie. In *Riders to the Sea* Cailteen advises Maura to go down to intercept Bartley at the 'spring well', and then 'the dark word will be broken'. Maura, however, was so /27/ astonished by the spectre of Michael that she could not give Bartley her protective blessing.

In choosing to abandon the 'black birds' and Martinmas motifs and replace them with 'ghost horse' and Samhain ones, Synge obviously intended to emphasize less the finality of death and slaughter than the world of spectre and spirit. Thus in the later drafts of the play Michael's (or Micheal's) body is discovered before cock-crow, (when apparitions are all banished). Nora tells Cailteen that the young priest said:

> 'There were two men,' says he, 'and they rowing round with poteen before the cocks crowed and the oar of one of them caught the body, and they passing the black cliffs of the North.'

In classical mythology there is a place of darkness through which spirits pass into Hades. Black cliffs occur as ominous places in many folk-tales and myths.

This, of course, connects up with the appearance later in the play of Michael's apparition, riding a grey pony. The colour grey is associated with death in Ireland. The Grey Washer by the Ford is, in Irish folk Tale, a female spectre who seems at first to be washing clothes in a river, but when approached by the man about to die she holds up the clothes and they have become the man's own phantom marked with the mortal wounds he is about to receive. Here the use of clothing and spectre echoes Synge's treatment of the appearance of Michael. It should be pointed out that in *Revelations* VI. 8. 'The Pale Horse' stands for Death, that Sleipnir, Odin's grey horse typified the wild wind, and that as Poseidon, the sea-god created the horse, so horse-farmers must be regarded as servants of Poseidon (or possibly of the moon-goddess, Demeter, to whom horses were also sacred). /28/

That Synge was aware of the universal nature of the symbolism he was using, can hardly be doubted. In a review of H. d'Arbois de Jubainville's *The Irish Mythological Cycle and Celtic Mythology* in *The Speaker* of 2 April 1904 Synge reveals his long-time familarity with this material and refers to the 'Greek kinship of these Irish legends' and illustrates his comment by suggesting that Lug is a Celtic Hermes and Balor the Chimaera. He also mentions 'Manannan mac Lir, an Irish sea god'. In an earlier review of Lady Gregory's *Cuchulain of Muirthemne* in *The Speaker* of 17 June 1902, Synge again compares Celtic with Homeric story, and here he says 'The Elizabethan vocabulary has a force and colour that makes it the only form of English that is quite suitable for incidents of the epic kind, and in her intercourse with the peasants of the west Lady Gregory has learned to use this vocabulary in a new way, while she carries with her plaintive Gaelic constructions that make her language, in a true sense, a language of Ireland.' This pasage indicates pretty clearly what Synge was about when he filled *Riders to the Sea* with mythic intimations and reveals also that, even while he was concerned to present accurately the life and dignity of the Aran peasant, he was also interested in creating a more universal picture of man surrounded by natural elements and supernatural forces—or beliefs about those supernatural forces—which he is unable to control.

Seen from this viewpoint, *Riders to the Sea* takes on something of a new identity. The very title itself emphasizes the mythic or super-natural element for there are only two riders in the play, one the doomed Bartley and the other his spectral brother. We are all, Maura tells us, doomed to death, for 'no man at all can be living for ever.' We all, await destruction. It is one of the messages of Greek Tragedy and the form of the play has much in common with the Greek theatre. The /29/ climactic action takes place off-stage and is com-mented upon by Maura, who returns, distraught with her forebodings as the Greek chorus returns similarly distraught in so many plays. The old women keening just before the news of Bartley's death is told, function like a Greek chorus as also do the two women who describe Bartley's death. In the Houghton typescript, which is prob-ably an earlier version than the established text, the stage directions give their speeches under the heading 'WOMEN' rather than ONE OF THE WOMEN which is the heading in all published versions.

The dramatic irony in the play is also similar to that found in Greek tragedy. Nora reports the priest's words thus: 'she'll be getting her death' says he 'with crying and lamenting': it is, indeed, Maura's lamenting Bartley's going down to the ship that prevents her from giving him her blessing and thus causes his death. A simpler, but still classical, use of foreboding speech occurs when Maura says to Bartley:

> 'It's hard set we'll be surely the day you've drowned with the rest what way will I live and the girls with me and I an old woman looking for the grave

After a further passage of foreboding, irony returns with a play upon the vernacular usage of the word 'destroyed'. Nora says:

> And it's destroyed he'll be going till dark night, and he after eating nothing since the sun went up.

Cailteen reinforces the effect:

> It's destroyed he'll be, surely.

The pathos and dignity of Maura's speech on taking Michael's stick to assist her steps as she goes to the spring to give her /30/ blessing to Bartley is not unlike many of the laments in Aeschylus, Sophocles, and Euripides:

> In the big world the old people do be leaving things after them for their sons and children, but in this place it is the young men do be leaving things behind them for them that do be old.

The emphasis in this speech upon the way in which the world of Maura differs from the 'big world' appears to set the island community apart from all other communities. Moreover, while in Greek Tragedy and Story the suffering of the protagonists is the consequence of the sins they or their kin have committed intentionally or otherwise, in *Riders to the Sea* there appears to be no reason for Maura's tribulation. The deaths of her sons are not, as are the deaths of Niobe's children, or Medea's, the consequence of acts of blasphemy or evil. In this, *Riders to the Sea* is closer to the world of Sophocles than Euripides; there is an arbitrary quality about the fates of the characters that reminds one of the world of Oedipus. Even there, however, one can find some historical justification for the cruelty of the fates. In *Riders to the Sea,* however, there is no justification. This is not a place in which there is any kind of justice, or mercy. The priest may say that 'the Almighty God won't leave her [Maura] destitute with no son living', but Maura tells us 'It's little the like of him knows of the sea.' The sea is, indeed, the 'Almighty God' of the play, an older and more formidable spiritual power than that represented by the priest who, it is emphasized, is 'young'. The priest never enters the action of the play. He is absent physically from the cottage of Maura just as he is, spiritually, a stranger to her world. His reported words are all comforting, but they do not comfort. /31/

Yet, it may be suggested that the Christianity plays a part in the play. Does not Maura sprinkle 'Holy Water' over the clothes of the drowned Michael?

This may be so, but there is some doubt as to the nature of that 'Holy Water' for Maura refers to 'going down and getting Holy Water in the dark nights after Samhain'. It may be that she collects it from a Holy Well, even the Spring Well mentioned in the play, but it is clear that the only time she does collect it is in the nights after Samhain, for now that Samhain is nearly come round again her supply is almost exhausted; it is the last of the Holy Water she sprinkles over Michael's clothes. Thus the Holy Water is much more the magical water of pre-christian belief than the water blessed by the priest. Indeed, the priest is not in it at all.

The fusion of pre-christian and christian belief is characteristic, of course, of many peasant communities. Synge was not playing fast and loose with the facts. He was, however, portraying a world in which people, insecure and desperate for help against the forces of death

and the tyranny of the natural world, seized upon any belief or superstition that might give them comfort and help. That Maura finds no
comfort or hope for all her observances is the dark message of the
play, which ends as a cry, not against God, but against the principle
of Mortality. 'No man can be living for ever and we must be satisfied.'

If this humble, even partly stoic, conclusion of Maura's is set against
the conclusion of Yeats's *Cathleen ni Houlihan,* together with all the
other elements in the play that I have mentioned, it becomes clear in
just what way *Riders to the Sea* is a counter-blast to Yeats. Synge was
certainly very much aware that his view of Ireland differed from that
of Yeats. Some of his poems, as I have suggested earlier, seem to be
/32/ retorts to Yeats's early lyrics. On 12 September 1907 he wrote, in
a letter to the Irish-American journalist, Frederick J. Gregg: 'I am
half inclined to try a play on "Deirdre"—it would be amusing to
compare it with Yeats's and Russell's . . .' *Deirdre of the Sorrows* is,
certainly, in many ways constructed so as to oppose the vision of
Yeats with another. It is therefore not unreasonable to look again at
Riders to the Sea in these terms.

Cathleen ni Houlihan is, of course, a personification of Ireland, an
old woman (the Shan Van Vocht) who has the 'walk of a queen.'
Maura, also an old woman, is not an allegorical but a typical figure;
she too mourns the past dead though her walk is not that of a queen,
but weak with age. Cathleen ni Houlihan mourns the loss of her 'four
fields'—the four provinces of Ireland. Maura mourns the loss of her
eight men-folk, but without the triumphant tone of Yeats's Old
Woman. The ship that brings hope of Irish freedom to Yeats's characters, brings death to the characters of Synge. *Riders to the Sea* is,
indeed, a comprehensive drama. It includes, at a more profound level
than *Cathleen ni Houlihan,* an awareness of the Irish inheritance of
story and belief. Its portrait of the island is that of a place shut off
from the 'big world', as Ireland itself is shut off. It is a portrait of a
place bewildered by two cultures, the ancient and the new, and by
two visions of the nature of the spiritual world.

The island of *Riders to the Sea* is Ireland, but more than Ireland.
Its predicaments are those of the Irish peasant, but also those of all
men subject to the tyranny of forces they do not understand. Its
beliefs are those of the Irish peasant, but they are also those of all
people who combine superstition with Christian belief, or who are
troubled by thoughts of spiritual realities beyond their ability to
understand and /33/ control. *Riders to the Sea* is not naturalistic
theatre; it is poetic theatre, and it is epic. The figure of man placed
against the power of the gods who destroy him is a main theme of

epic and of heroic tragedy. Maura, like Oedipus, bows to the will of the gods, and, like Job, finds at last in humanity and endurance a dignity and greatness of spirit, turning down the empty cup of holy water in a last symbolic gesture, and asking for mercy upon the souls of all mortal kind.

Suggestions for Papers

Short Papers

Answer James Joyce's criticisms of *Riders to the Sea* as found in the selections from Ellmann and Joyce. (See also "Introduction.")

Evaluate Robin Skelton's contention, based on a comparison of *Cathleen ni Houlihan* and *Riders to the Sea*, that the latter is a "counterblast to Yeats."

Contrast *Riders to the Sea* and W. B. Yeats's *The Only Jealousy of Emer.*

Develop the comparison suggested by Donna Gerstenberger between *Riders to the Sea* and García Lorca's *Blood Wedding.*

Develop Denis Johnston's suggestion of a comparison between *Riders to the Sea* and Samuel Beckett's *Waiting for Godot.*

Is *Riders to the Sea* a "static drama"? See Price, Gerstenberger, and Levitt.

By a comparison of the language of *Riders to the Sea* and that of *The Playboy of the Western World*, support Van Laan's contention that in the former, because of its brevity, Synge restricts "his natural lyric bent."

Imagine yourself a director explaining how one or more of the characters in *Riders to the Sea* should be conceived and acted.

Develop the theme of dream versus actuality which Alan Price finds in *Riders to the Sea.*

Develop Donna Gerstenberger's objection to placing *Riders to the Sea* in the same category as W. B. Yeats's *The Shadowy Waters.*

Evaluate Denis Johnston's contrast of *Riders to the Sea* with the Faust legend. See also Thomas Van Laan's reference to Marlowe's *Dr. Faustus.*

Discuss the implications of the title of the play, including the biblical allusions which Levitt sees in it.

Are the characters in *Riders to the Sea* too passive in their suffering?

Is the catastrophe of *Riders to the Sea* too accidental?

How convincing is the use of the supernatural in *Riders to the Sea?*

Discuss the peculiar conditions of the struggle between youth and age in *Riders to the Sea.*

Develop Denis Donoghue's comparison of the use of the sea in *Riders to the Sea* with the use of the forest in Eugene O'Neill's *The Emperor Jones.*

Explain how Synge could have ruined *Riders to the Sea,* pointing out possible plot elements which he did *not* put in.

If there is heroism in *Riders to the Sea,* how does the play define it?

Trace the imagery of white and black in *Riders to the Sea.*

What is the final attitude toward life communicated by *Riders to the Sea?*

Long Papers

Is *Riders to the Sea* really a tragedy? See "Introduction," Ellmann, Bourgeois, Joyce, Donoghue, Price, Van Laan, Gerstenberger, Johnston, and Skelton.

Compare and contrast the interpretations advanced by Van Laan and Donoghue with regard to the theme of Christian acceptance in *Riders to the Sea.*

Discuss the function of the Christian imagery in the play, taking into account the views of Price, Gerstenberger, Johnston, and Levitt.

Evaluate Jan Setterquist's thesis that *Riders to the Sea* is reminiscent of Henrik Ibsen, taking into account the comments of Donoghue and Van Laan on *Rosmersholm.*

Discuss the characterization in *Riders to the Sea,* taking into account the argument developed most fully by R. L. Collins, but found also in Donoghue, Van Laan, and Gerstenberger (in contrast to Price), that Synge suppresses individual personality in this play.

Taking into account what is said by Donoghue, Price, Van Laan, Levitt, and (especially) Gerstenberger, discuss the use of symbolic stage picture in *Riders to the Sea*.

Discuss the structural organization of *Riders to the Sea*, taking account of the views of Price, Van Laan, Johnston, and Levitt.

Contrast the emphasis on imagery of Christian myth in Levitt's essay with the emphasis on imagery of pagan myth in Skelton's essay.

Discuss the brevity of *Riders to the Sea* and the distinction between actual and dramatic time, taking account of the remarks on this subject in Ellmann, Joyce, Van Laan, and Levitt.

Discuss the symbolism of the sea in *Riders to the Sea*, taking account of what is said by Bourgeois, Donoghue, Setterquist, Van Laan, Gerstenberger, and Skelton.

Is *Riders to the Sea* a Maeterlinckean drama? See Bourgeois and Gerstenberger and some of the work of Maurice Maeterlinck.

Is there suspense in *Riders to the Sea*? See Price, Van Laan, Johnston, and Levitt.

Discuss what Bourgeois calls "the exact nature and origin of Synge's conception of fate." See also Donoghue, Setterquist, Van Laan, Gerstenberger, Johnston, Levitt, and Skelton.

Do you find more realism or symbolism in *Riders to the Sea*? (See Bourgeois, Collins, Setterquist, Price, Van Laan, Gerstenberger, Levitt, and Skelton for symbolic use of realistic details.)

Additional Readings

The most complete accurate and fully annotated collection of Synge's work is *J. M. Synge: Collected Works*. General Editor: Robin Skelton. Volume I. *Poems*. Edited by Robin Skelton. London: Oxford University Press, 1962. Volume II. *Prose*. Edited by Alan Price. 1966 Volume III. *Plays*. Book I. Edited by Ann Saddlemyer. 1968. Volume IV. *Plays*. Book II. Edited by Ann Saddlemyer. 1968.

Books

Corkery, Daniel. *Synge and Anglo-Irish Literature*. Dublin and Cork: Cork University Press; London: Longmans Green & Company, 1931.

Ellis-Fermor, Una. *The Irish Dramatic Movement*. London: Methuen & Co., 1939.

Figgis, Darrel. *Studies and Appreciations*. London: Dent & Company, 1912.

Greene, David H. and Edward M. Stephens. *J. M. Synge, 1871-1909*. New York: The Macmillan Company, 1959.

Gregory, Lady Augusta. *Our Irish Theatre*. New York: G. P. Putnam's Sons, 1913.

Henn, T. R., editor. *The Plays and Poems of J. M. Synge*. London: Methuen & Co., 1963.

Howarth, Herbert. *The Irish Writers: Literature and Nationalism, 1880-1940*. New York: Hill and Wang, 1959.

Kenny, Edward. *The Splendid Years: Recollections of Maire Nic Shiubhlaigh; as told to Edward Kenny*. Dublin: J. Duffy, 1955.

Lucas, F. L. *The Drama of Chekhov, Synge, Yeats, and Pirandello*. London: Cassell & Co., 1963.

O Síocháin, P. A. *Aran: Islands of Legend*. Dublin: Foilsiúcháin Éireann, 1962.

Robinson, Lennox. *Ireland's Abbey Theatre: A History, 1899-1951*. London: Sidgwick and Jackson, 1951.

Skelton, Robin and Ann Saddlemyer, editors. *The World of W. B. Yeats: Essays in Perspective.* Victoria, B. C.: The Adelphi Book Shop for the University of Victoria, 1965.

Strong, L. A. G. *John Millington Synge.* London: Allen & Unwin, 1941.

Taylor, Estella Ruth. *The Modern Irish Writers: Cross Currents of Criticism.* Lawrence: The University of Kansas Press, 1954.

Williams, Raymond. *Drama from Ibsen to Eliot.* London: Chatto and Windus, 1952.

Yeats, W. B. *The Autobiography of William Butler Yeats.* New York: The Macmillan Company, 1938.

_____. *Essays and Introductions.* New York: The Macmillan Company, 1961.

_____. *Explorations.* Selected by Mrs. W. B. Yeats. New York: The Macmillan Company, 1962.

Articles

Combs, William W. "J. M. Synge's *Riders to the Sea*: A Reading and Some Generalizations," *Publications of the Michigan Academy of Science, Arts and Letters,* L (1965), 599-607.

Fausset, Hugh I'A. "Synge and Tragedy," *The Fortnightly Review,* No. DCLXXXVI, n. s. (February 1, 1924), 256-73.

General Instructions
for a Research Paper

If your instructor gives you any specific directions about the format of your research paper that differ from the directions given here, you are, of course, to follow his directions. Otherwise, you can observe these directions with the confidence that they represent fairly standard conventions.

A research paper represents a student's synthesis of his reading in a number of primary and secondary works, with an indication, in footnotes, of the source of quotations used in the paper or of facts cited in paraphrased material. A *primary* source is the text of a work as it issued from the pen of the author or some document contemporary with the work. The following, for instance, would be considered primary sources: a manuscript copy of the work; first editions of the work and any subsequent editions authorized by the writer; a modern scholarly edition of the text; an author's comment about his work in letters, memoirs, diaries, journals, or periodicals; published comments on the work by the author's contemporaries. A *secondary* source would be any interpretation, explication, or evaluation of the work printed, usually several years after the author's death, in critical articles and books, in literary histories, and in biographies of the author. In this casebook, the text of the work, any variant versions of it, any commentary on the work by the author himself or his contemporaries may be considered as primary sources; the editor's Introduction, the articles from journals, and the excerpts from books are to be considered secondary sources. The paper that you eventually write will become a secondary source.

Plagiarism

The cardinal sin in the academic community is plagiarism. The rankest form of plagiarism is the verbatim reproduction of someone else's words without any indication that the passage is a quotation. A lesser but still serious form of plagiarism is to report, in your own

129

words, the fruits of someone else's research without acknowledging the source of your information or interpretation.

You can take this as an inflexible rule: every verbatim quotation in your paper must be either enclosed in quotation marks or single-spaced and inset from the left-hand margin and must be followed by a footnote number. Students who merely change a few words or phrases in a quotation and present the passage as their own work are still guilty of plagiarism. Passages of genuine paraphrase must be footnoted too if the information or idea or interpretation contained in the paraphrase cannot be presumed to be known by ordinary educated people or at least by readers who would be interested in the subject you are writing about.

The penalties for plagiarism are usually very severe. Don't run the risk of a failing grade on the paper or even of a failing grade in the course.

Lead-Ins

Provide a lead-in for all quotations. Failure to do so results in a serious breakdown in coherence. The lead-in should at least name the person who is being quoted. The ideal lead-in, however, is one that not only names the person but indicates the pertinence of the quotation.

Examples:

    (typical lead-in for a single-spaced, inset quotation)

    Irving Babbitt makes this observation about
    Flaubert's attitude toward women:

(typical lead-in for quotation worked into the frame of one's sentence)

    Thus the poet sets out to show how the present
    age, as George Anderson puts it, "negates the
    values of the earlier revolution."[7]

Full Names

The first time you mention anyone in a paper give the full name of the person. Subsequently you may refer to him by his last name.

Examples: First allusion—Ronald S. Crane
               Subsequent allusions—Professor Crane,
               as Crane says.

Ellipses

Lacunae in a direct quotation are indicated with *three spaced periods,* in addition to whatever punctuation mark was in the text at the point where you truncated the quotation. *Hit the space-bar of your type-writer between each period.* Usually there is no need to put the ellipsis-periods at the beginning or the end of a quotation.

Example: "The poets were not striving to communi-
cate with their audience; . . . By and
large, the Romantics were seeking . . .
to express their unique personalities."[8]

Brackets

Brackets are used to enclose any material interpolated into a direct quotation. The abbreviation *sic,* enclosed in brackets, indicates that the error of spelling, grammar, or fact in a direct quotation has been copied as it was in the source being quoted. If your typewriter does not have special keys for brackets, draw the brackets neatly with a pen.

Examples: "He [Theodore Baum] maintained that Con-
fucianism [the primary element in Chinese
philosophy] aimed at teaching each individual to accept his lot in life."[12]

"Paul Revear [sic] made his historic ride
on April 18, 1875 [sic]."[15]

Summary Footnote

A footnote number at the end of a sentence which is not enclosed in quotation marks indicates that only *that* sentence is being documented in the footnote. If you want to indicate that the footnote documents more than one sentence, put a footnote number at the end of the *first* sentence of the paraphrased passage and use some formula like this in the footnote:

[16] For the information presented in this and the
following paragraph, I am indebted to Marvin
Magalaner, Time of Apprenticeship: the Fiction of
Young James Joyce (London, 1959), pp. 81-93.

Citing the Edition

The edition of the author's work being used in a paper should always be cited in the first footnote that documents a quotation from that work. You can obviate the need for subsequent footnotes to that edition by using some formula like this:

⁴ Nathaniel Hawthorne, "Young Goodman Brown," as printed in <u>Young Goodman Brown</u>, ed. Thomas E. Connolly, Charles E. Merrill Literary Casebooks (Columbus, Ohio, 1968), pp. 3-15. This edition will be used throughout the paper, and hereafter all quotations from this book will be documented with a page-number in parentheses at the end of the quotation.

Notetaking

Although all the material you use in your paper may be contained in this casebook, you will find it easier to organize your paper if you work from notes written on 3 x 5 or 4 x 6 cards. Besides, you should get practice in the kind of notetaking you will have to do for other term-papers, when you will have to work from books and articles in, or on loan from, the library.

An ideal note is a self-contained note—one which has all the information you would need if you used anything from that note in your paper. A note will be self-contained if it carries the following information:

(1) The information or quotation *accurately* copied.
(2) Some system for distinguishing direct quotation from para-phrase.
(3) All the bibliographical information necessary for documenting that note—full name of the author, title, volume number (if any), place of publication, publisher, publication date, page numbers.
(4) If a question covered more than one page in the source, the note-card should indicate which part of the quotation occurred on one page and which part occurred on the next page. The easiest way to do this is to put the next page number in paren-theses after the last word on one page and before the first word on the next page.

In short, your note should be so complete that you would never have to go back to the original source to gather any piece of information about that note.

Footnote Forms

The footnote forms used here follow the conventions set forth in the *MLA Style Sheet,* Revised Edition, ed. William Riley Parker, which is now used by more than 100 journals and more than thirty university presses in the United States. Copies of this pamphlet can be purchased for fifty cents from your university bookstore or from the Modern Language Association, 62 Fifth Avenue, New York, New York 10011. If your teacher or your institution prescribes a modified form of this footnoting system, you should, of course, follow that system.

A primary footnote, the form used the first time a source is cited, supplies four pieces of information: (1) author's name, (2) title of the source, (3) publication information, (4) specific location in the source of the information or quotation. A secondary footnote is the shorthand form of documentation after the source has been cited in full the first time.

Your instructor may permit you to put all your footnotes on separate pages at the end of your paper. But he may want to give you practice in putting footnotes at the bottom of the page. Whether the footnotes are put at the end of the paper or at the bottom of the page, they should observe this format of spacing: (1) the first line of each footnote should be indented, usually the same number of spaces as your paragraph indentations; (2) all subsequent lines of the footnote should start at the lefthand margin; (3) there should be single-spacing within each footnote and double-spacing between each footnote.

Example:

[10] Ruth Wallerstein, *Richard Crashaw: A Study in Style and Poetic Development*, University of Wisconsin Studies in Language and Literature, No. 37 (Madison, 1935), p. 52.

Primary Footnotes

(The form to be used the *first* time a work is cited)

[1] Paull F. Baum, *Ten Studies in the Poetry of Matthew Arnold* (Durham, N.C., 1958), p. 37.

(book by a single author; p. is the abbreviation of *page*)

[2] René Wellek and Austin Warren, *Theory of Literature* (New York, 1949), pp. 106-7.

(book by two authors; pp. is the abbreviation of *pages*)

³ William Hickling Prescott, History of the Reign
of Philip the Second, King of Spain, ed. John Foster
Kirk (Philadelphia, 1871), II, 47.

(an edited work of more than one volume; *ed.* is the abbreviation
for "edited by"; note that whenever a volume number is cited, the
abbreviation p. or pp. is *not* used in front of the page number)

⁴ John Pick, ed., The Windhover (Columbus, Ohio,
1968), p. 4.

(form for quotation from an editor's Introduction—as, for instance,
in this casebook series; here *ed.* is the abbreviation for "editor")

⁵ A.S.P. Woodhouse, "Nature and Grace in The Faerie
Queen," in Elizabethan Poetry: Modern Essays in
Criticism, ed. Paul J. Alpers (New York, 1967),
pp. 346-7.

(chapter or article from an edited collection)

⁶ Morton D. Paley, "Tyger of Wrath," PMLA, LXXXI
(December, 1966), 544.

(an article from a periodical; note that because the volume number
is cited no p. or pp. precedes the page number; the titles of periodicals are often abbreviated in footnotes but are spelled out in the
Bibliography; here, for instance, *PMLA* is the abbreviation for
Publications of the Modern Language Association)

Secondary Footnotes

(Abbreviated footnote forms to be used after a work has been cited
once in full)

⁷ Baum, p. 45.

(abbreviated form for work cited in footnote #1; note that the
secondary footnote is indented the same number of spaces as the
first line of primary footnotes)

⁸ Wellek and Warren, pp. 239-40.

(abbreviated form for work cited in footnote #2)

⁹ Prescott, II, 239.

(abbreviated form for work cited in footnote #3; because this is
a multi-volume work, the volume number must be given in addition to the page number)

¹⁰ Ibid., p. 245.

(refers to the immediately preceding footnote—that is, to page
245 in the second volume of Prescott's history; *ibid.* is the abbre-

viation of the Latin adverb *ibidem* meaning "in the same place"; note that this abbreviation is italicized or underlined and that it is followed by a period, because it is an abbreviation)

[11] Ibid., III, 103.

(refers to the immediately preceding footnote—that is, to Prescott's work again; there must be added to *ibid.* only what changes from the preceding footnote; here the volume and page changed; note that there is no p. before 103, because a volume number was cited)

[12] Baum, pp. 47–50.

(refers to the same work cited in footnote #7 and ultimately to the work cited in full in footnote #1)

[13] Paley, p. 547.

(refers to the article cited in footnote #6)

[14] Rebecca P. Parkin, "Mythopoeic Activity in the Rape of the Lock," ELH, XXI (March, 1954), 32.

(since this article from the *Journal of English Literary History* has not been previously cited in full, it must be given in full here)

[15] Ibid., pp. 33–4.

(refers to Parkin's article in the immediately preceding footnote)

Bibliography Forms

Note carefully the differences in bibliography forms from footnote forms: (1) the last name of the author is given first, since bibliography items are arranged alphabetically according to the surname of the author (in the case of two or more authors of a work, only the name of the first author is reversed) ; (2) the first line of each bibliography item starts at the lefthand margin; subsequent lines are indented; (3) periods are used instead of commas, and parentheses do not enclose publication information; (4) the publisher is given in addition to the place of publication; (5) the first and last pages of articles and chapters are given; (6) most of the abbreviations used in footnotes are avoided in the Bibliography.

The items are arranged here alphabetically as they would appear in the Bibliography of your paper.

Baum, Paull F. Ten Studies in the Poetry of Matthew Arnold. Durham, N.C.: University of North Carolina Press, 1958.

Paley, Morton D. "Tyger of Wrath," Publications of
    the Modern Language Association, LXXXI (Decem-
    ber, 1966), 540-51.

Parkin, Rebecca P. "Mythopoeic Activity in the Rape
    of the Lock," Journal of English Literary
    History, XXI (March, 1954), 30-8.

Pick, John, editor. The Windhover. Columbus, Ohio:
    Charles E. Merrill Publishing Company, 1968.

Prescott, William Hickling. History of the Reign of
    Philip the Second, King of Spain. Edited by
    John Foster Kirk. 3 volumes. Philadelphia: J.B.
    Lippincott and Company, 1871.

Wellek, René and Austin Warren. Theory of Litera-
    ture. New York: Harcourt, Brace & World, Inc.,
    1949.

Woodhouse, A.S.P. "Nature and Grace in The Faerie
    Queene," in Elizabethan Poetry: Modern Essays in
    Criticism. Edited by Paul J. Alpers. New York:
    Oxford University Press, 1967, pp. 345-79.

If the form for some work that you are using in your paper is not given in these samples of footnote and bibliography entries, ask your instructor for advice as to the proper form.

Other Books by David R. Clark

A Curious Quire. Poems by Stanley Koehler, Leon O. Barron, David R. Clark, Robert G. Tucker. Lithographs by Donald R. Matheson. Amherst, 1962, 1967.

W. B. Yeats and the Theatre of Desolate Reality. Dublin, 1965; Chester Springs, Pa., 1965.

Irish Renaissance: A Gathering of Essays, Memoirs, and Letters from The Massachusetts Review. Edited by Robin Skelton and David R. Clark. Dublin, 1965.

Dry Tree. Poems by David R. Clark. Drawing by Bill Darr. Dublin, 1966.

Reading Poetry. Second Edition. By Fred B. Millett, Arthur W. Hoffman, and David R. Clark. New York, 1968.